52 FASCINATING

MERMAID LEGENDS

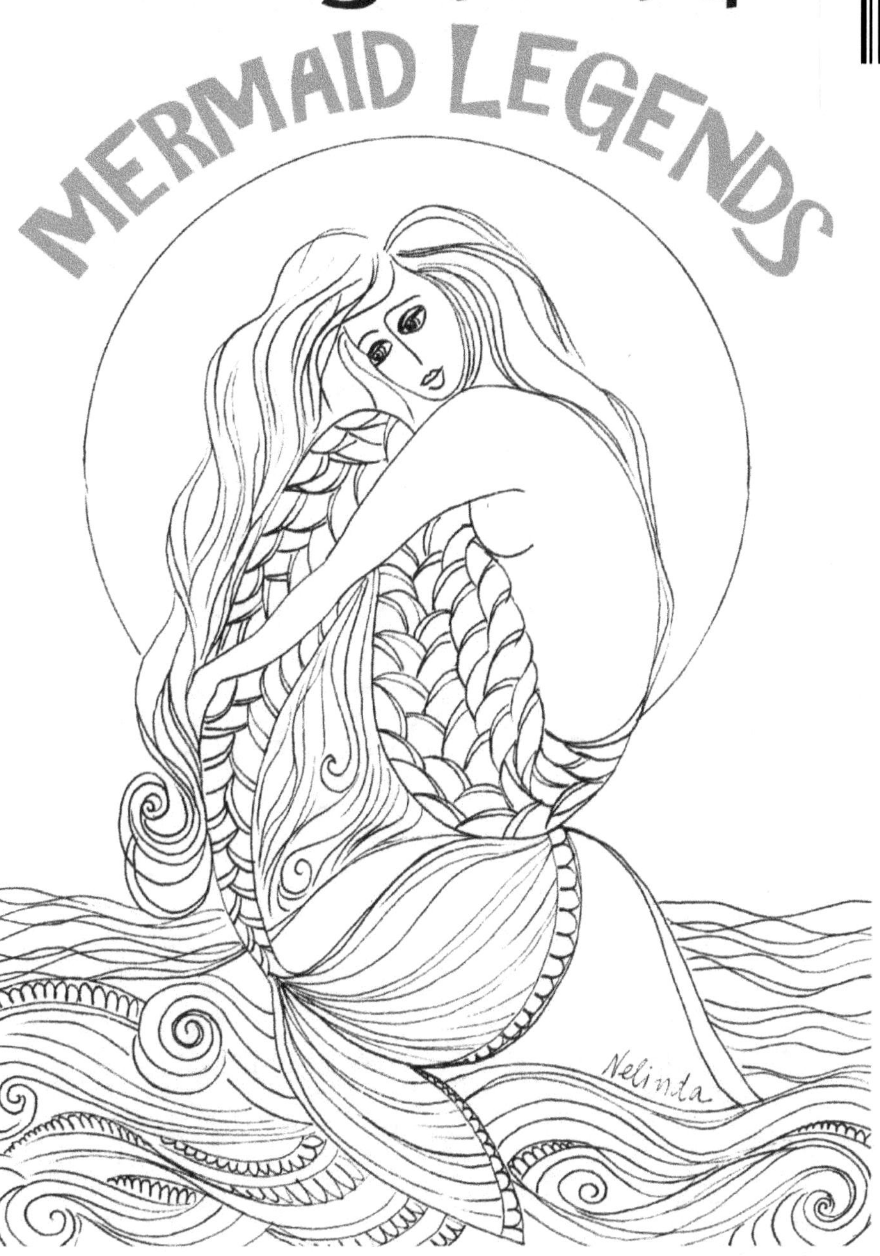

coloring book by Ronesa Aveela - illustrated by Nelinda

Introduction

Mankind's fascination with the sea has sparked imagination since the first person beheld its mighty waters. Curiosity led people to invent the means to travel across the great oceans and eventually explore beneath them, trying to discover their secrets. Throughout the centuries, millennia in fact, people have created myths and legends about creatures living within the sea's depths.

One of the most alluring and formidable beings to inspire writers, artists, children, and adults is the mermaid, who entices men to a watery death. Mermaids have existed in literature since 1000 BC where Assyrians worshiped this fin-tailed goddess of the moon. They have been forever immortalized in stories such as Hans Christian Andersen's "The Little Mermaid," but there is more to them than what that story tells.

Cultures across the globe tell tales of half-human, half-fish creatures who live in water. Some of them may wish to harm humans, while others prefer to help.

The coloring pages that follow give you a sprinkling of the types of mermaids you may find in different areas of the world, with a tidbit of information about them.

All are hand-drawn by artist Nelinda, then scanned into digital format. The rest is up to you to bring these wild, mysterious creatures to life using colors and your imagination.

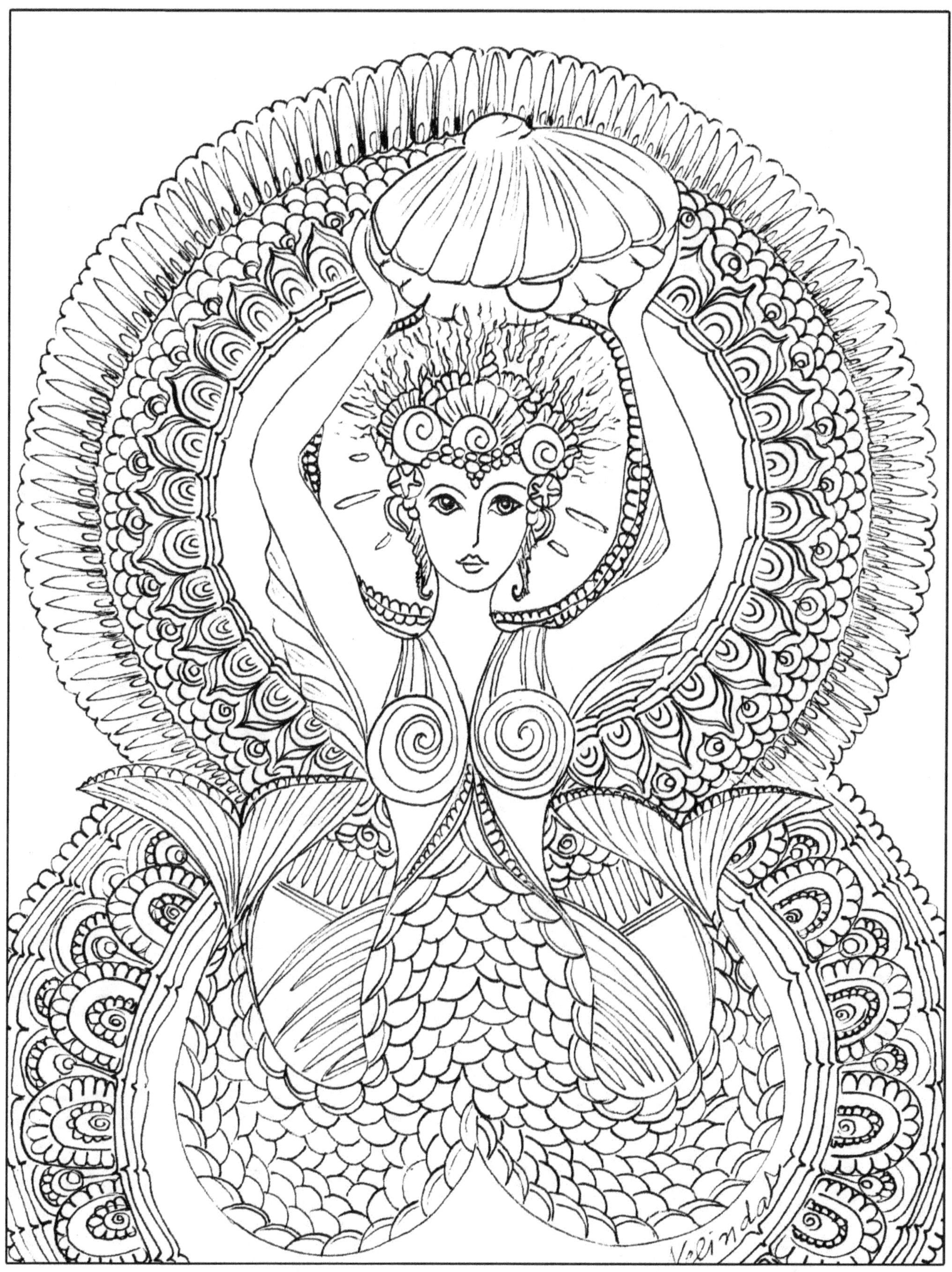

Atargatis – Assyria, 1000 BC. The first recorded mermaid. This moon goddess used moonlight mixed with silver to create the first mirror, which could look into the future or see into faraway lands.

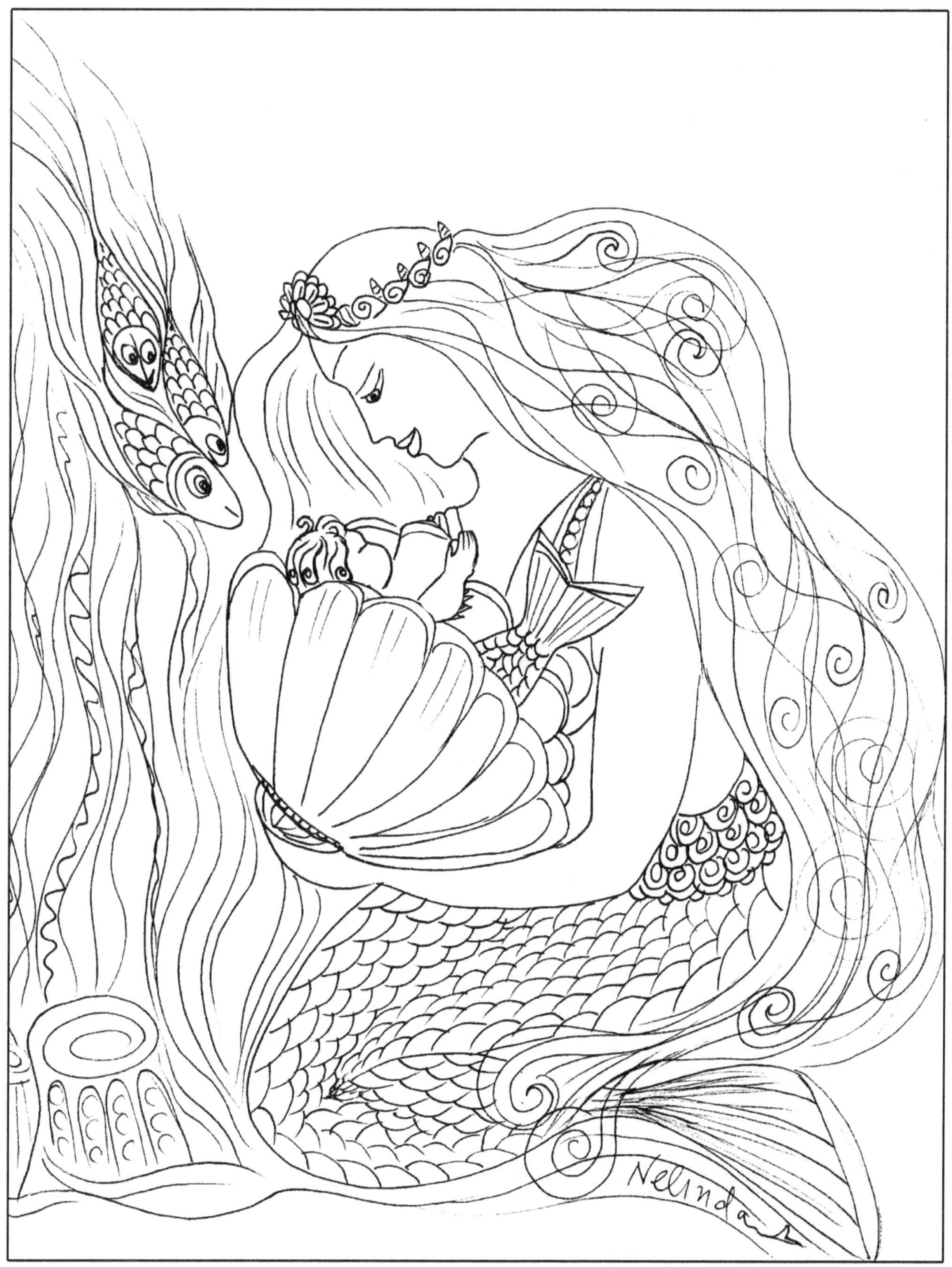

Yemoja – Nigeria. Her name means "mother whose children are like fish."
Yemanjá – Brazil. People who lose jewelry in the ocean consider it an offering to Yemanjá, who will bless them for the gift.

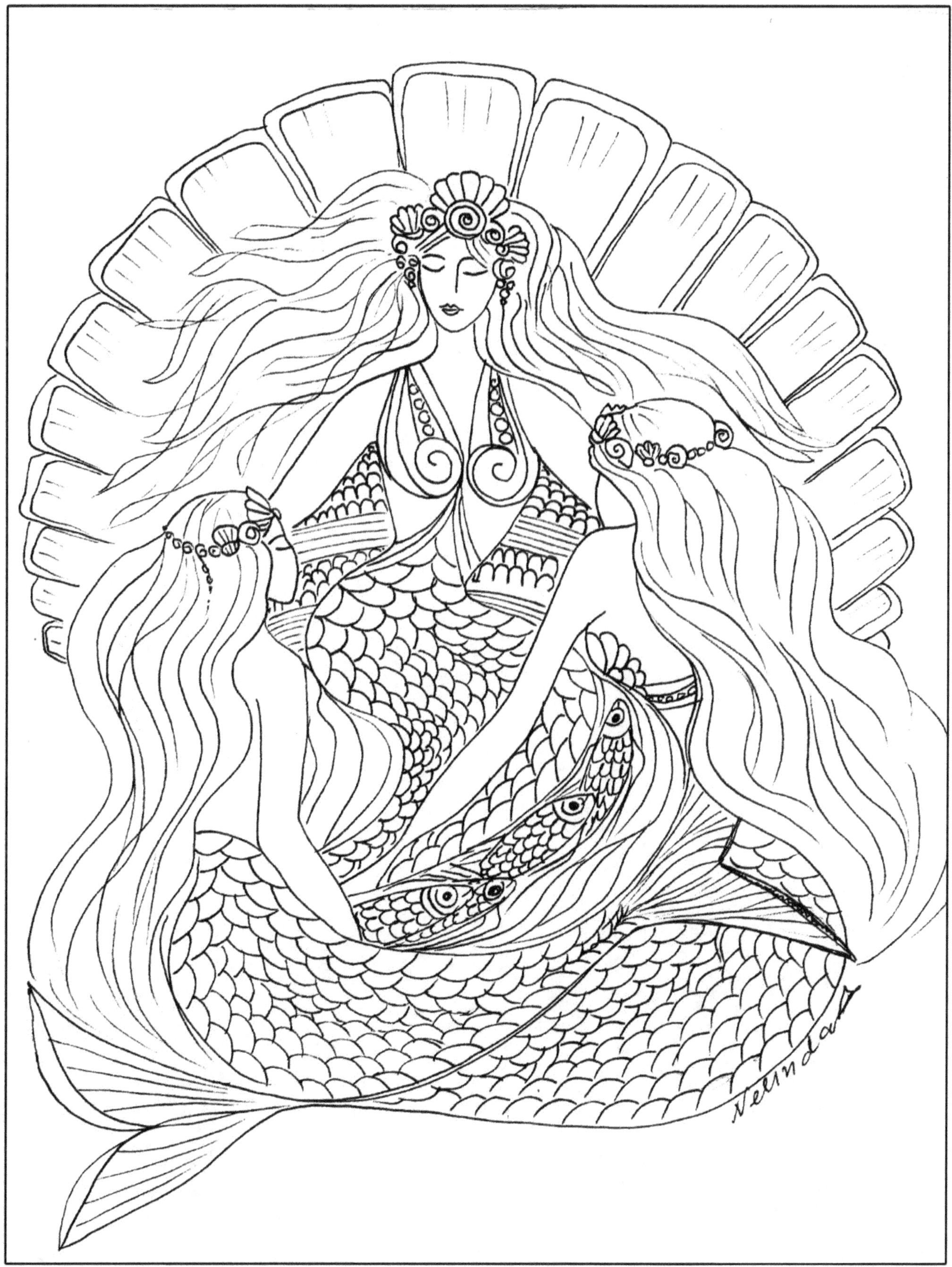

Derceto – ancient Palestine. This goddess of the moon and fertility was the Philistine version of the goddess Atargatis.

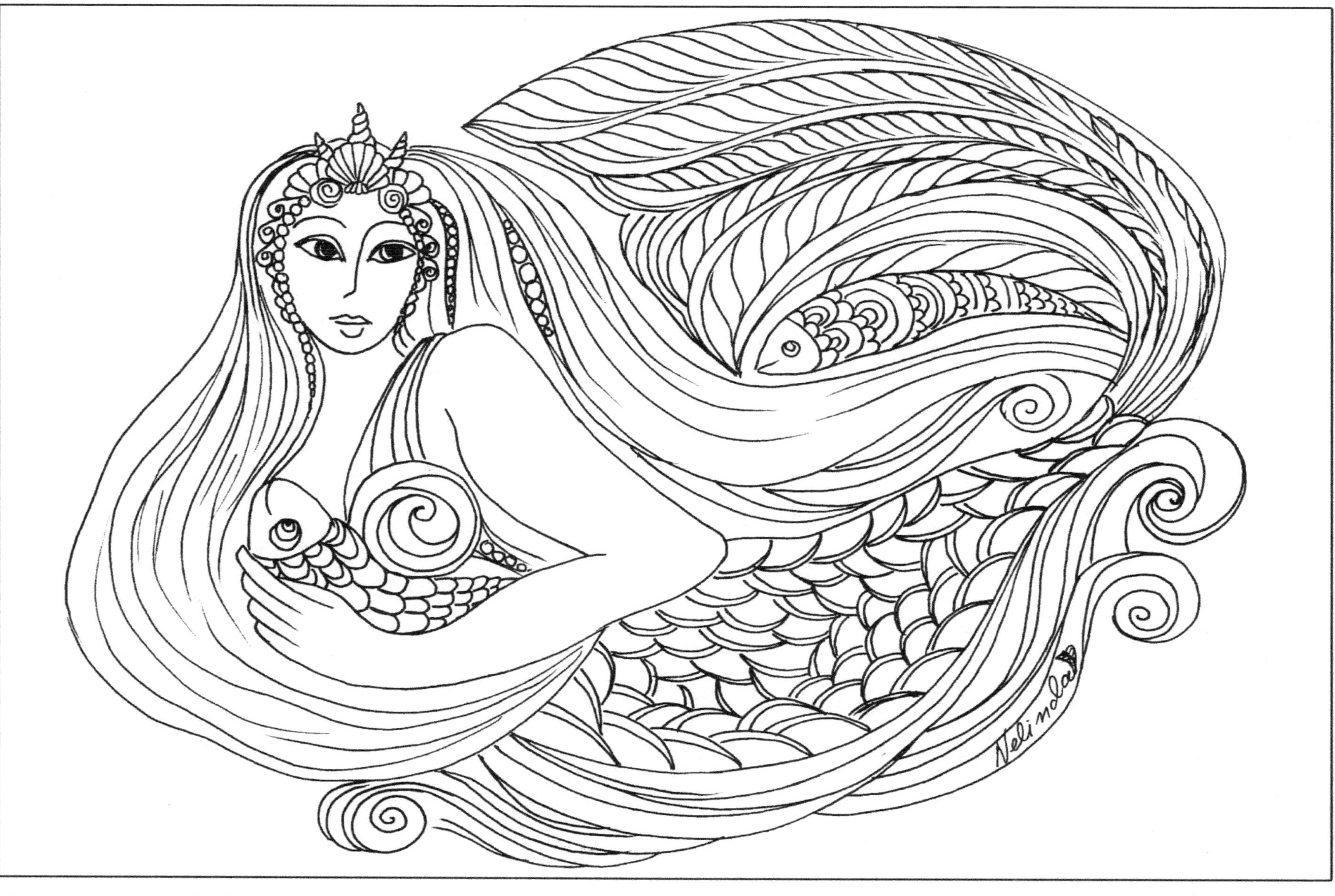

Merrows – Ireland. These green-haired or blonde beauties wore enchanted red-feather caps that allowed them to swim underwater.

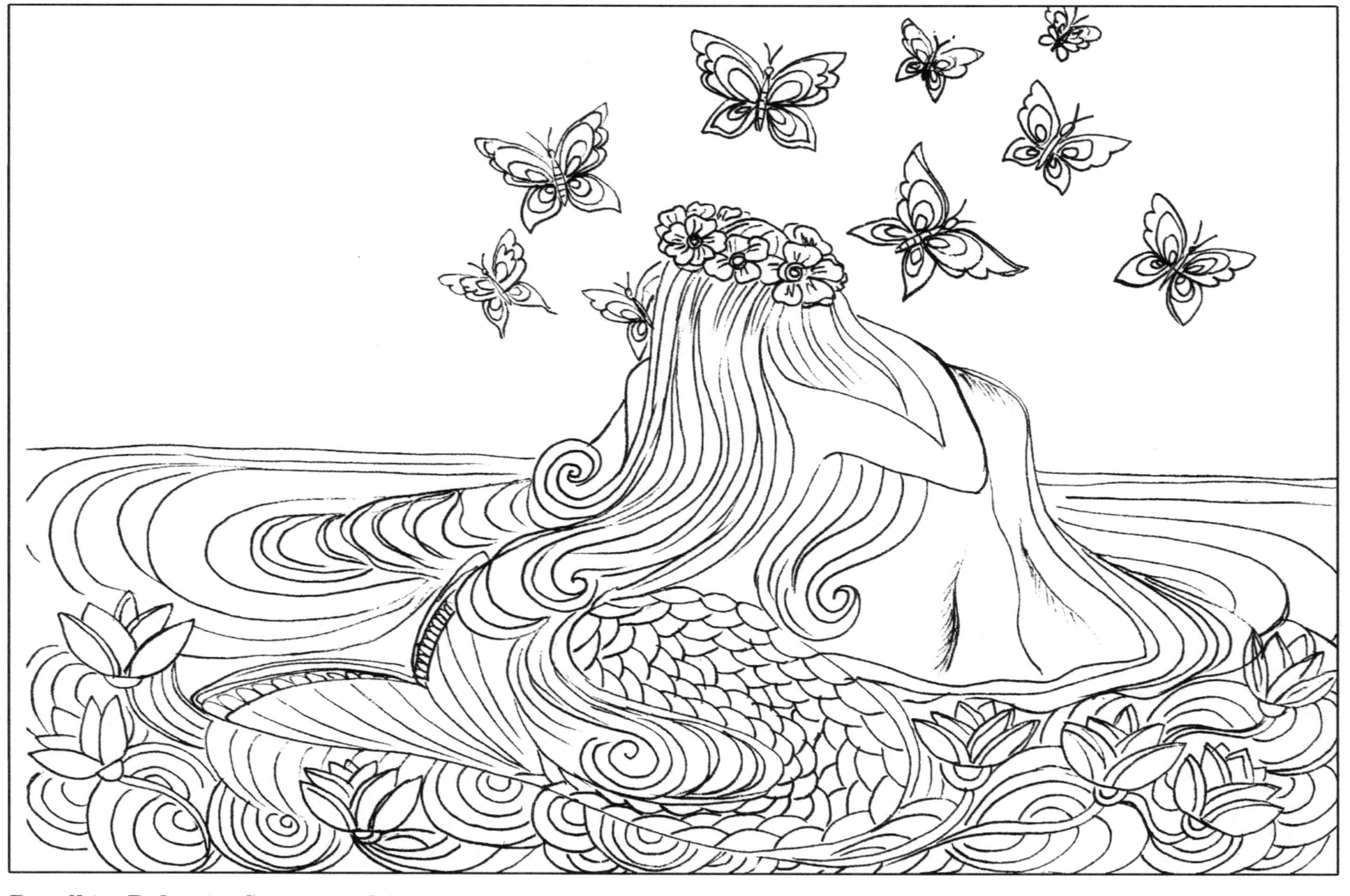

Rusalki – Bulgaria. Some say they are young women who have drowned. They appear at times as white or silver butterflies, the symbol of the soul.

www.ronesaavela.com

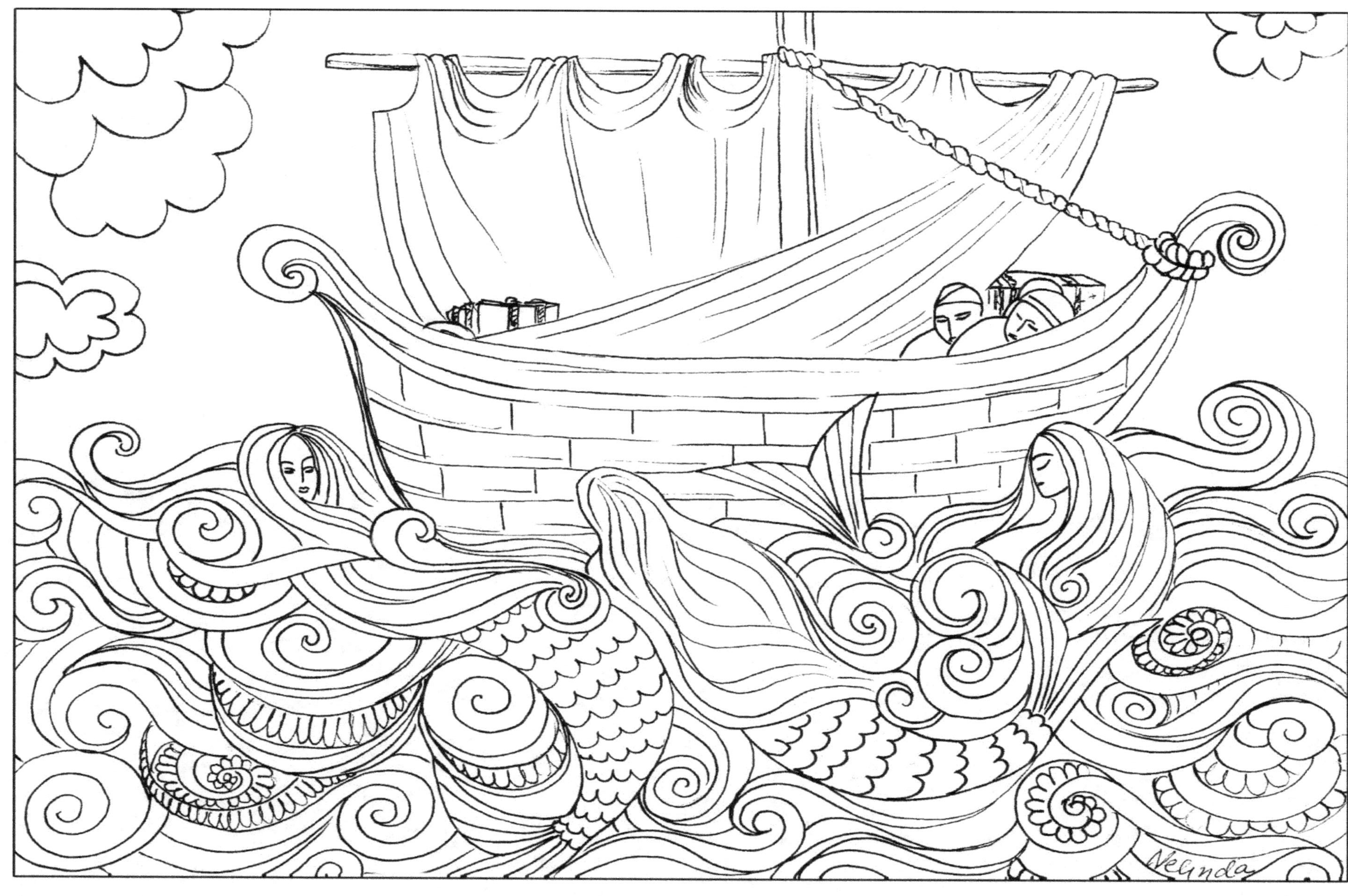

Sirens – Greece. They are best known for their songs that lured sailors toward rocky coasts, where shipwrecks and death awaited them.

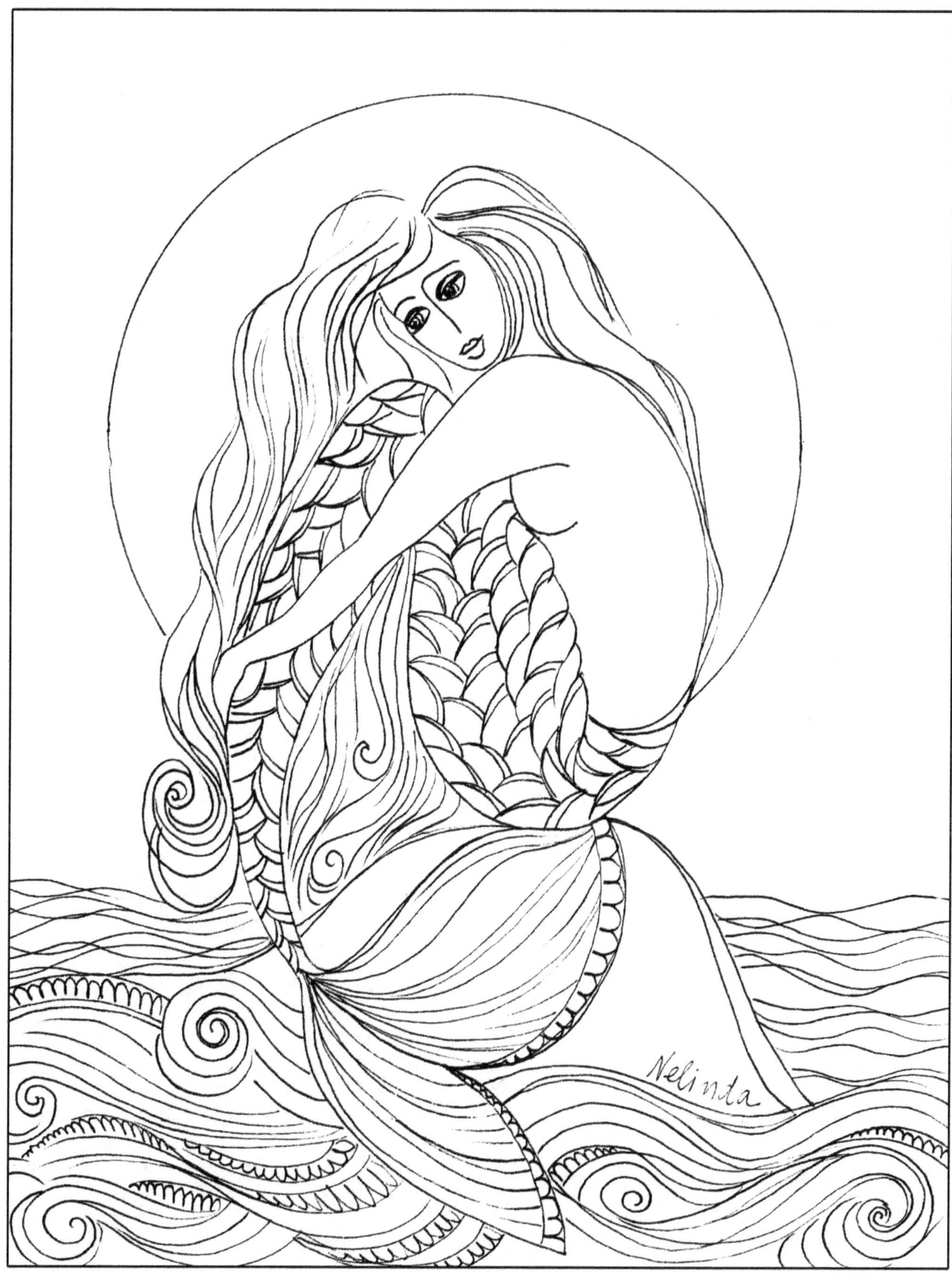

The Little Mermaid – Denmark. In the original version, when mermaids died, they turned into sea foam, unless a human promised to be true to them forever.

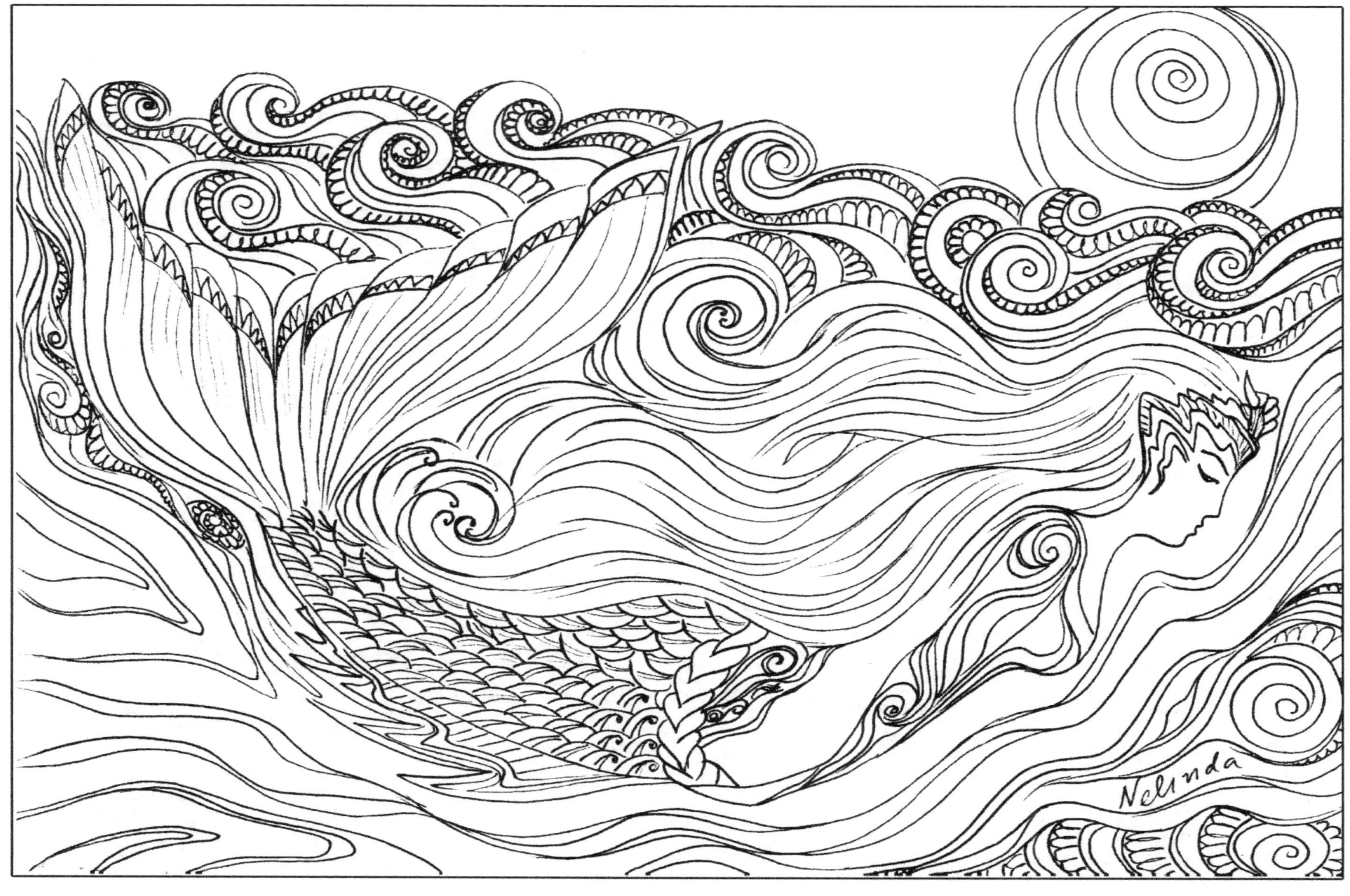

Menana of the Waterfall – Native American (Ottowa). Menana lived among the stars, then in water, and finally on land as half fish, half human—only to become fully human when a man could love her.

www.ronesaavela.com

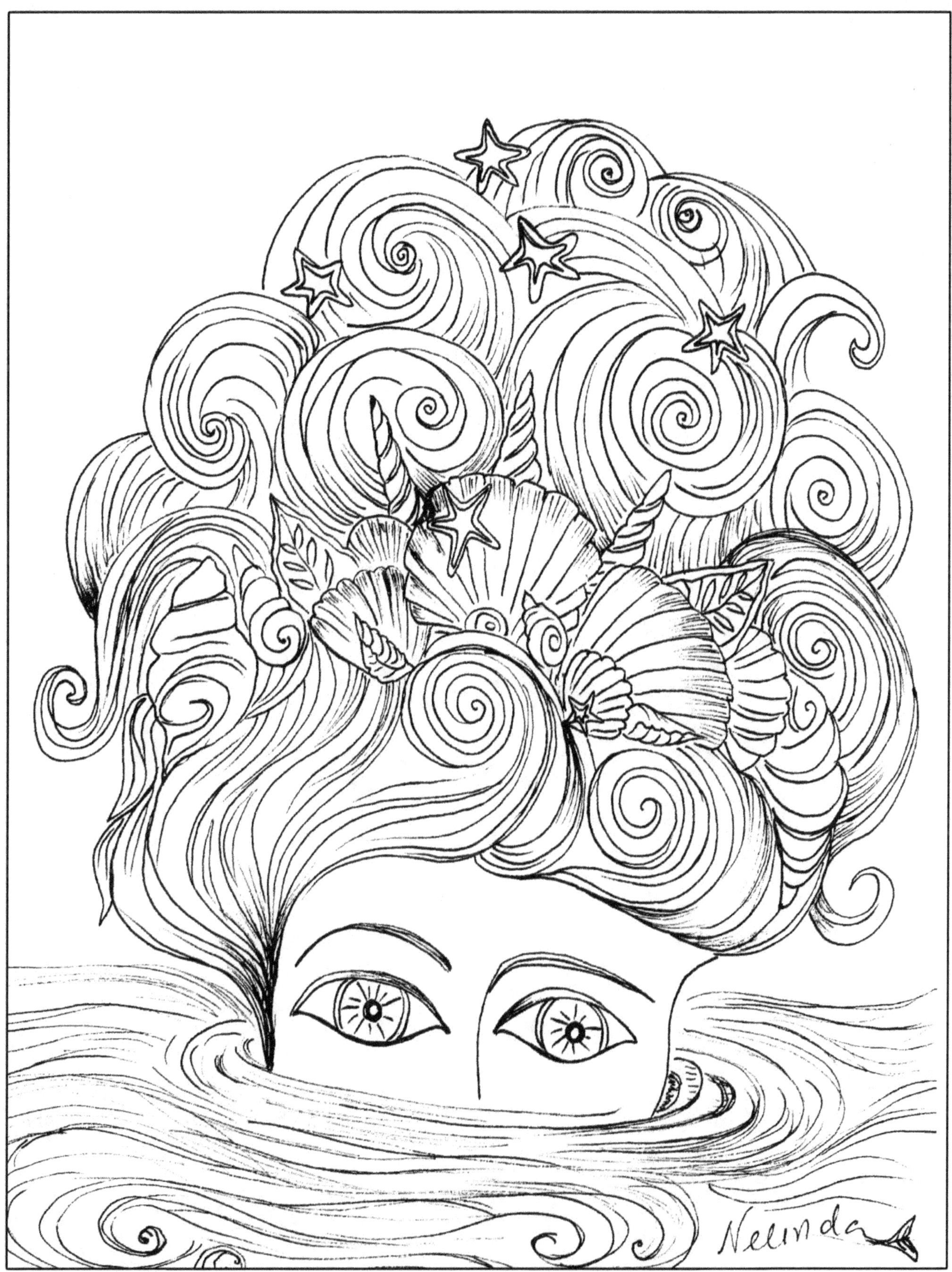

The Siren Wife – Italy. A sailor throws his unfaithful wife into the sea, where she becomes a Siren. They both regret their actions and find a way to be together again.

www.ronesaavela.com

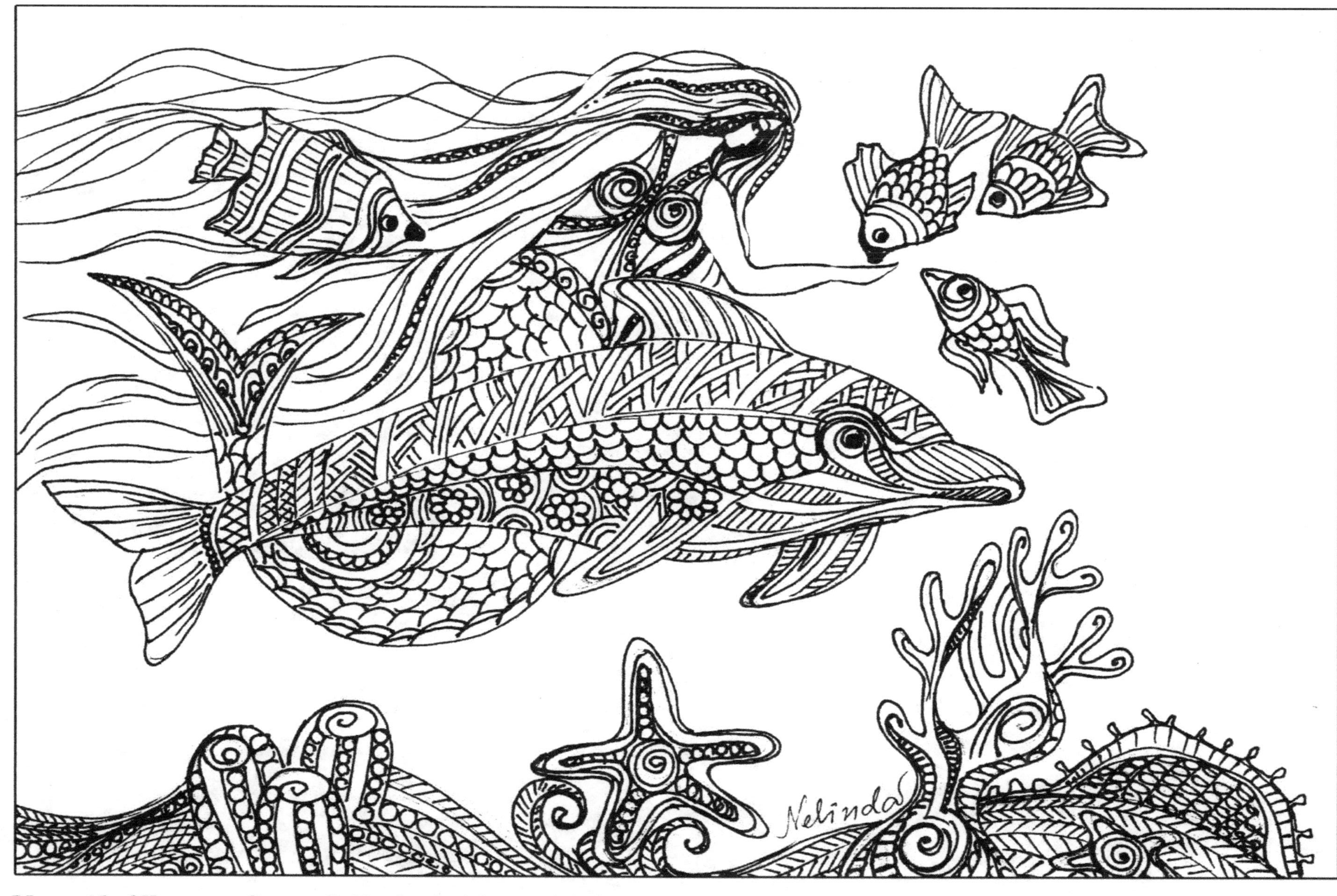

Mermaid of Zennor – Cornwall, England. A beautiful church lady with an enchanting singing voice lures away a prominent church member to be her husband under the sea.

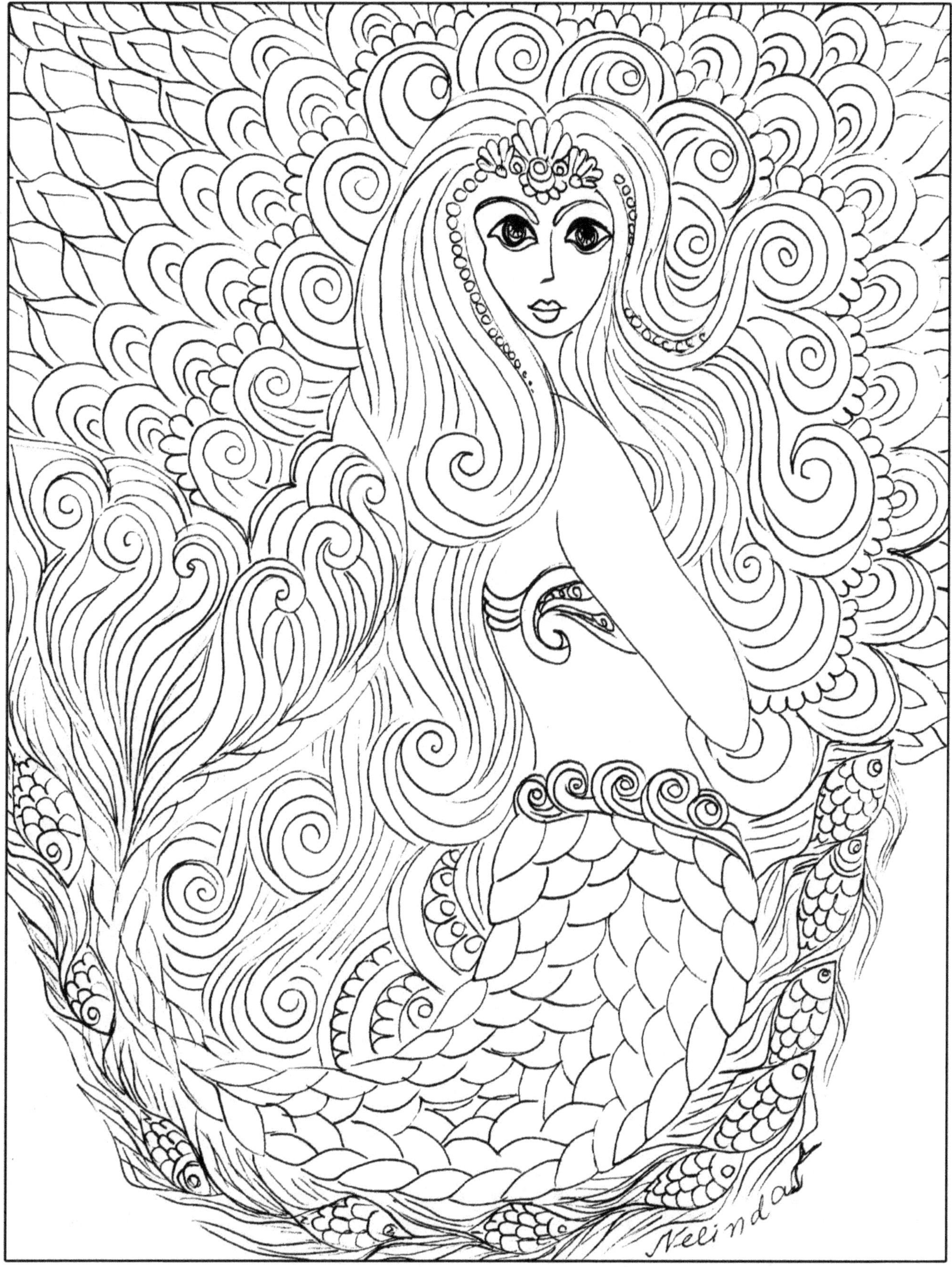

Pania of the Reef – New Zealand. A Maori legend says that when the mermaid Pania tried to return to her human husband, the sea people turned her into a reef.

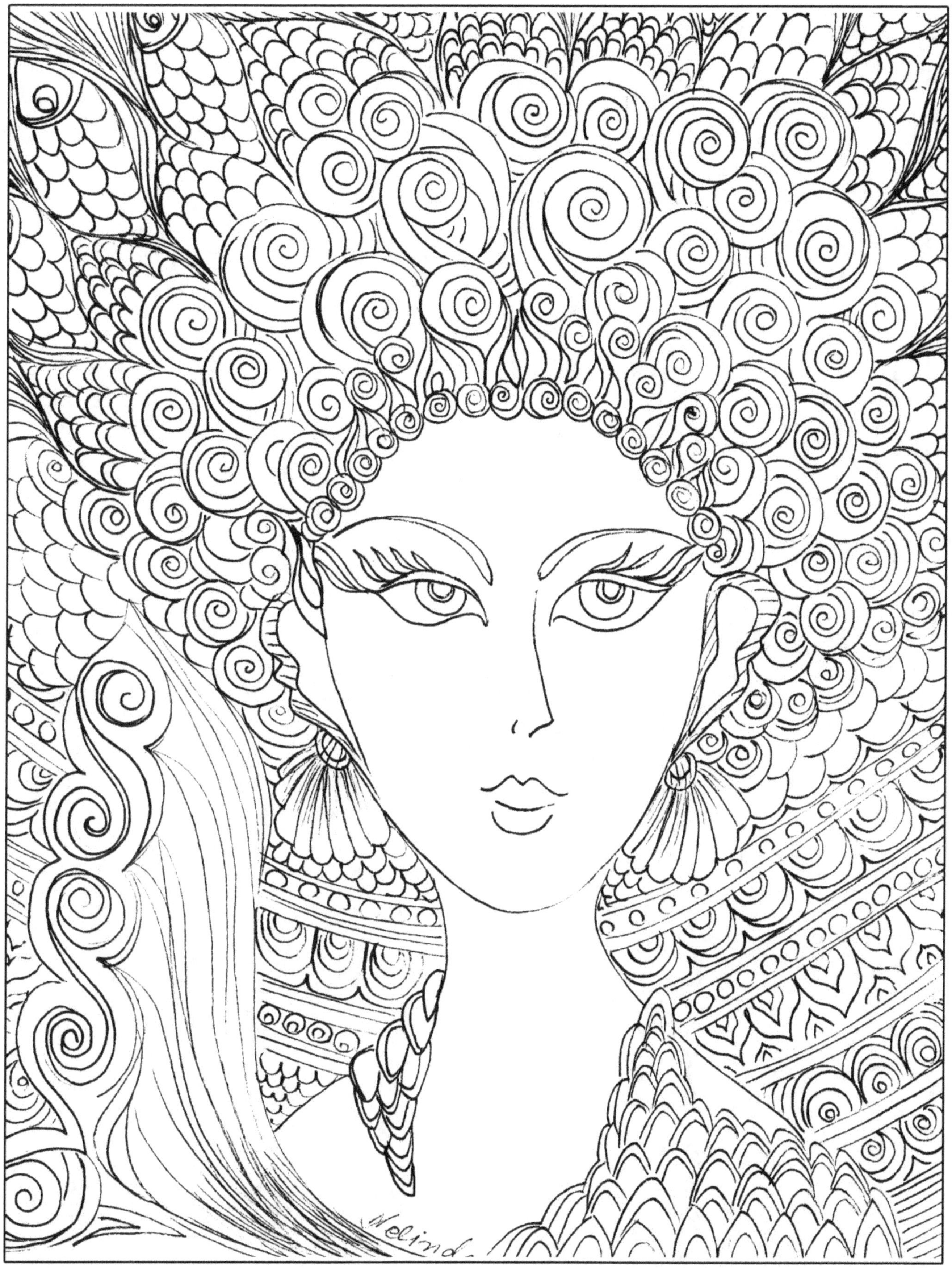

Melusina – France. Cursed by her mother to be a serpent from the waist down on Saturdays, Melusina had to find a husband who would vow to never see her on Saturday.

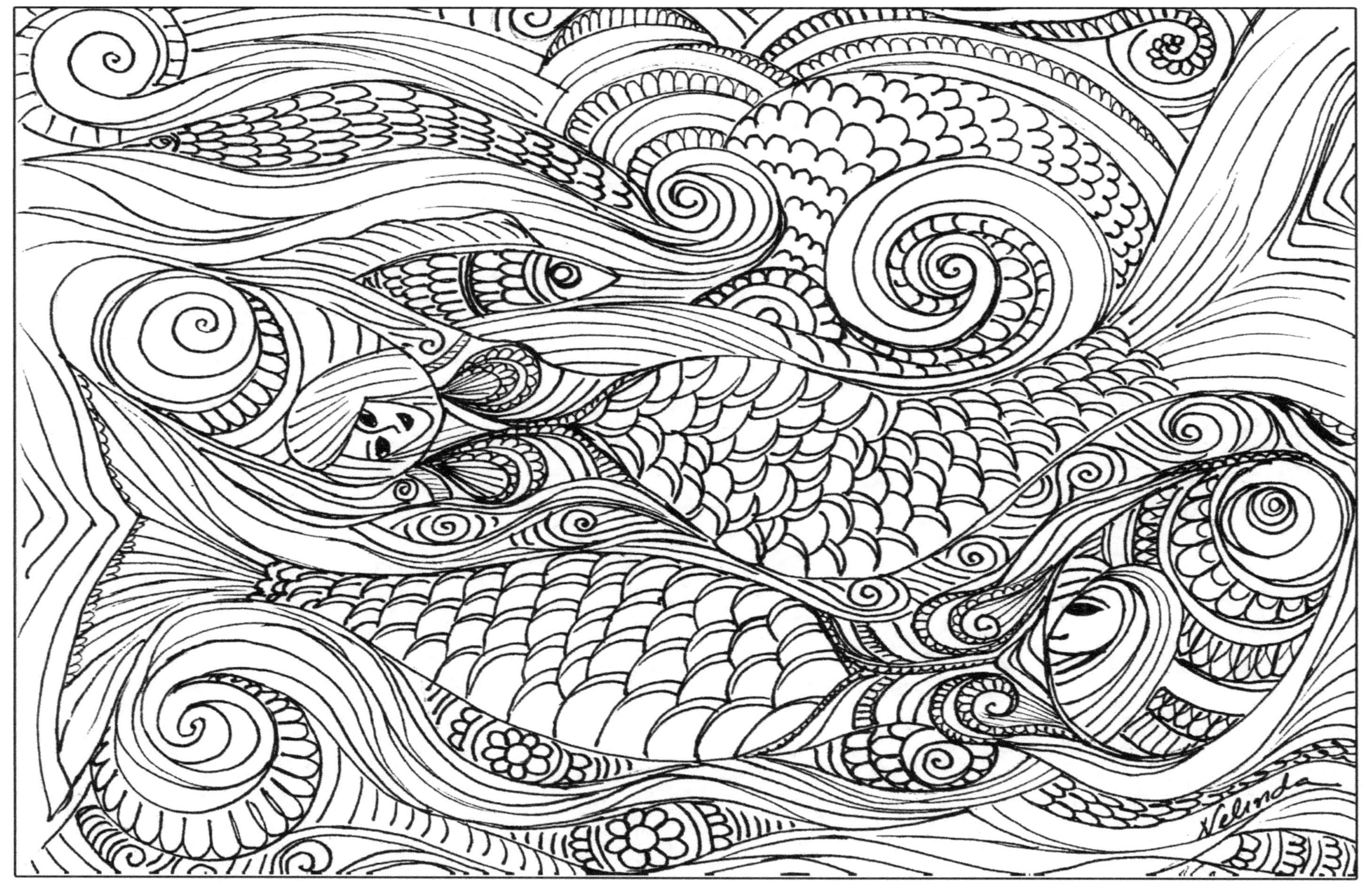

LaSiren and LaBalenn – Haiti. The two sisters represent the ocean and women's personality. LaSiren is strong and fumes like fire like the ocean's surface, while LaBalenn is cold and calm like the ocean depths.

www.ronesaavela.com

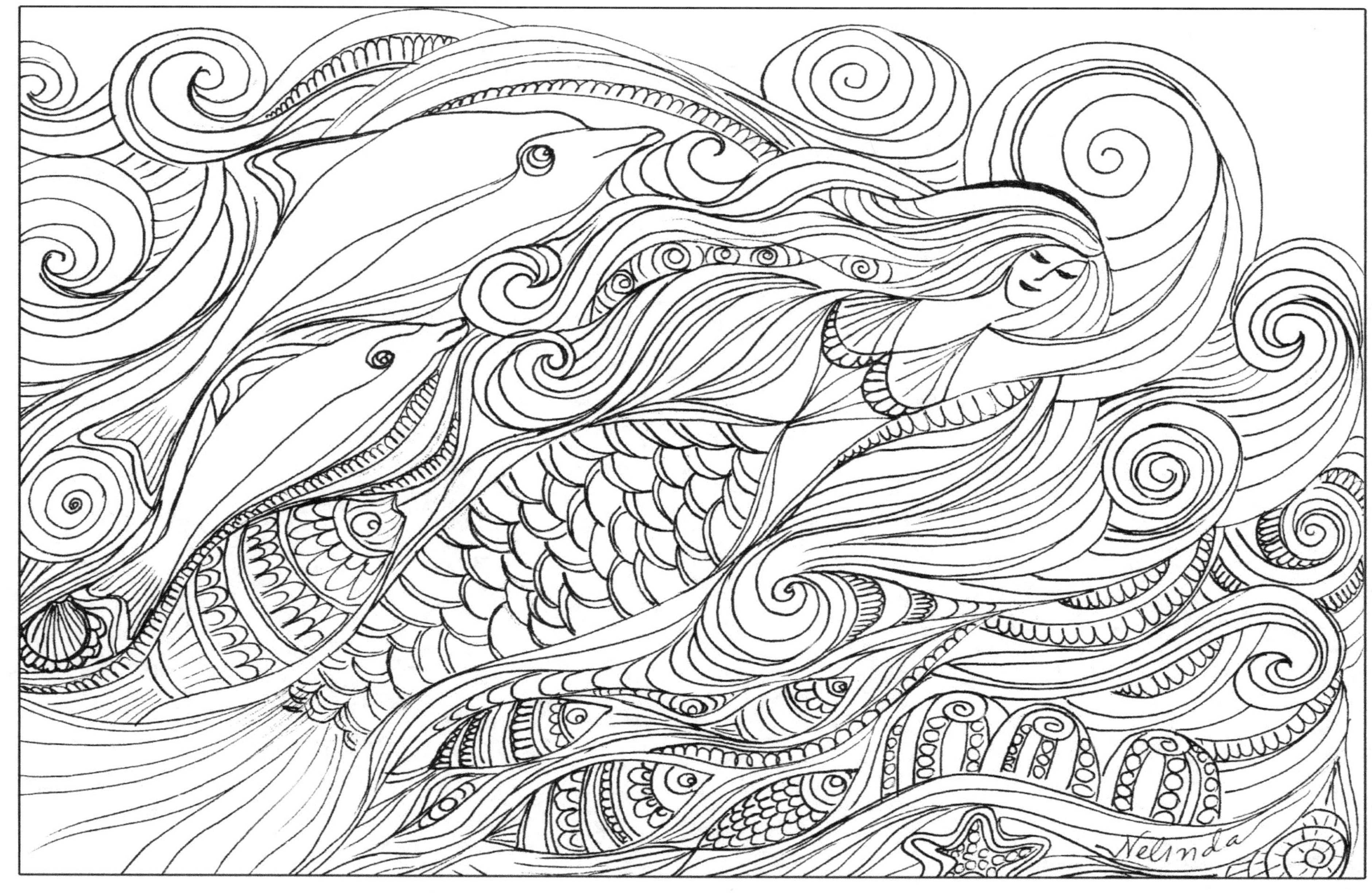

Sedna – Canada. In this Inuit tale, a father tosses his daughter overboard and cuts off her fingers as she clings to the side. They become fish, seals, walruses, and whales.

www.ronesaavela.com

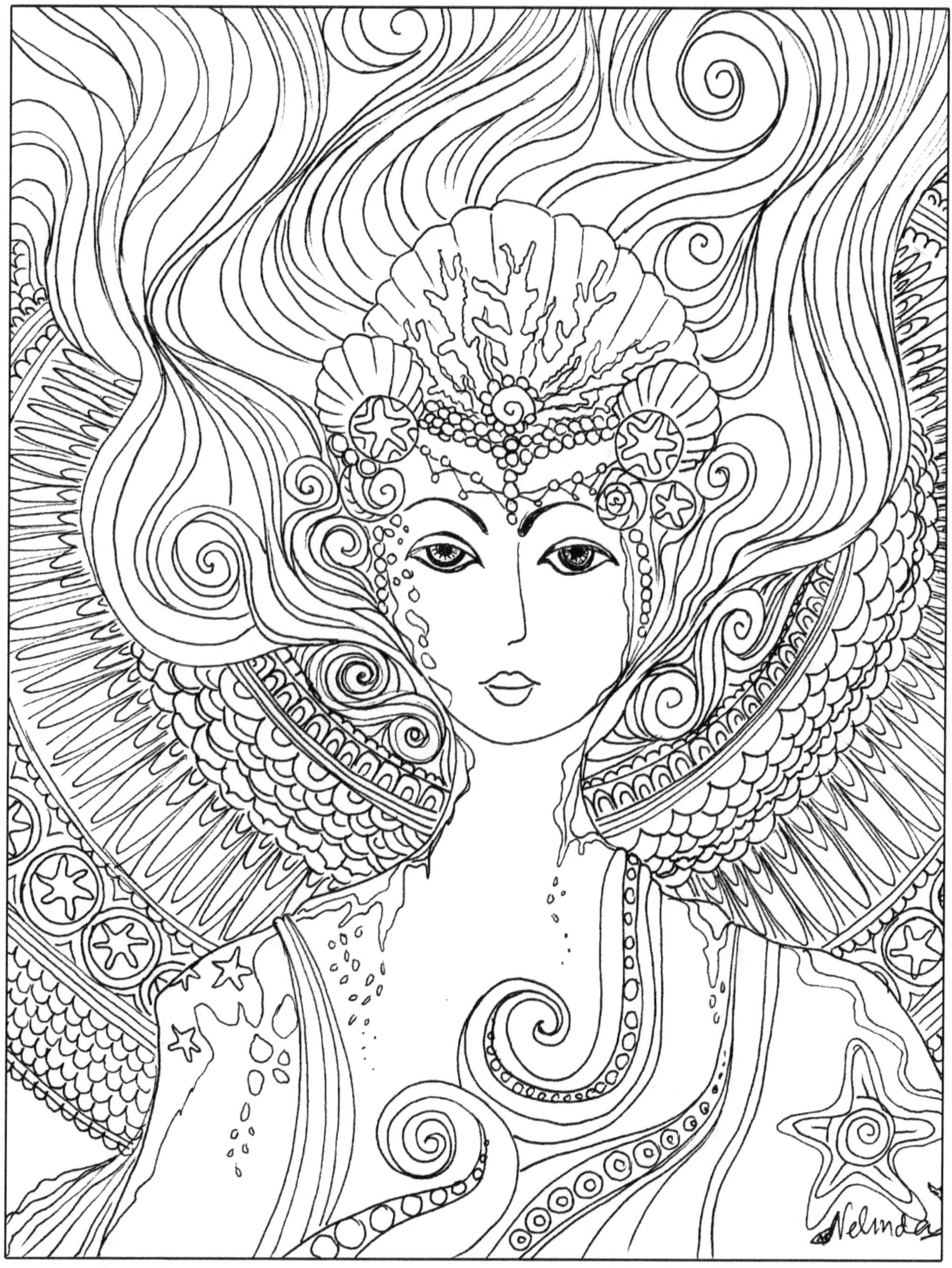

Mami Wata – Africa. This water spirit is often seen with one or two large snakes (of rebirth and healing) wrapped around her body. Human knowledge of healing was believed to come from fairies or mermaids.

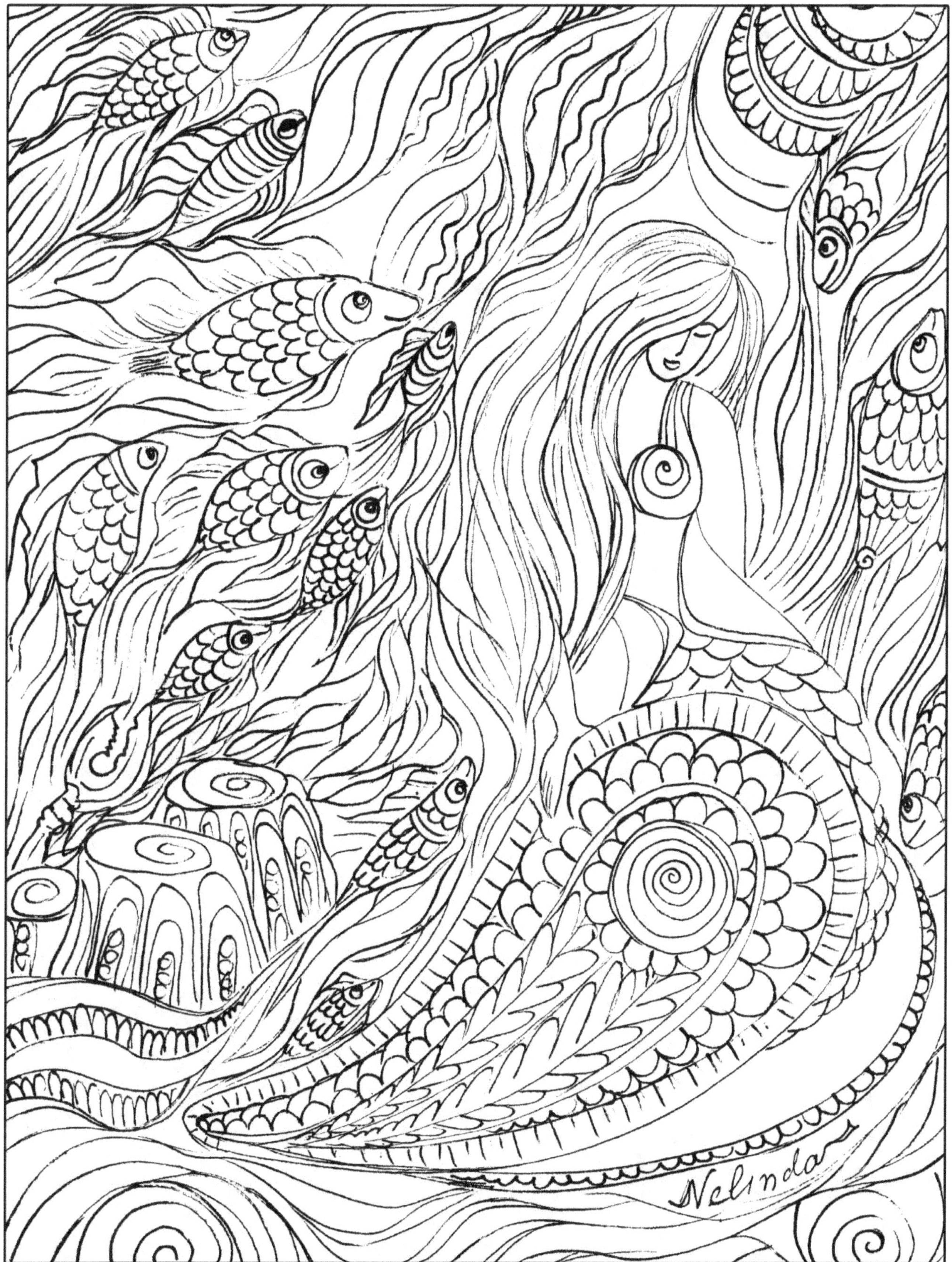

River Mumma – Jamaica. In the depths of the sea, she guards the Golden Table left by the Spaniards. If anyone tries to steal it when it rises to the surface, she pulls them into the water and drowns them.

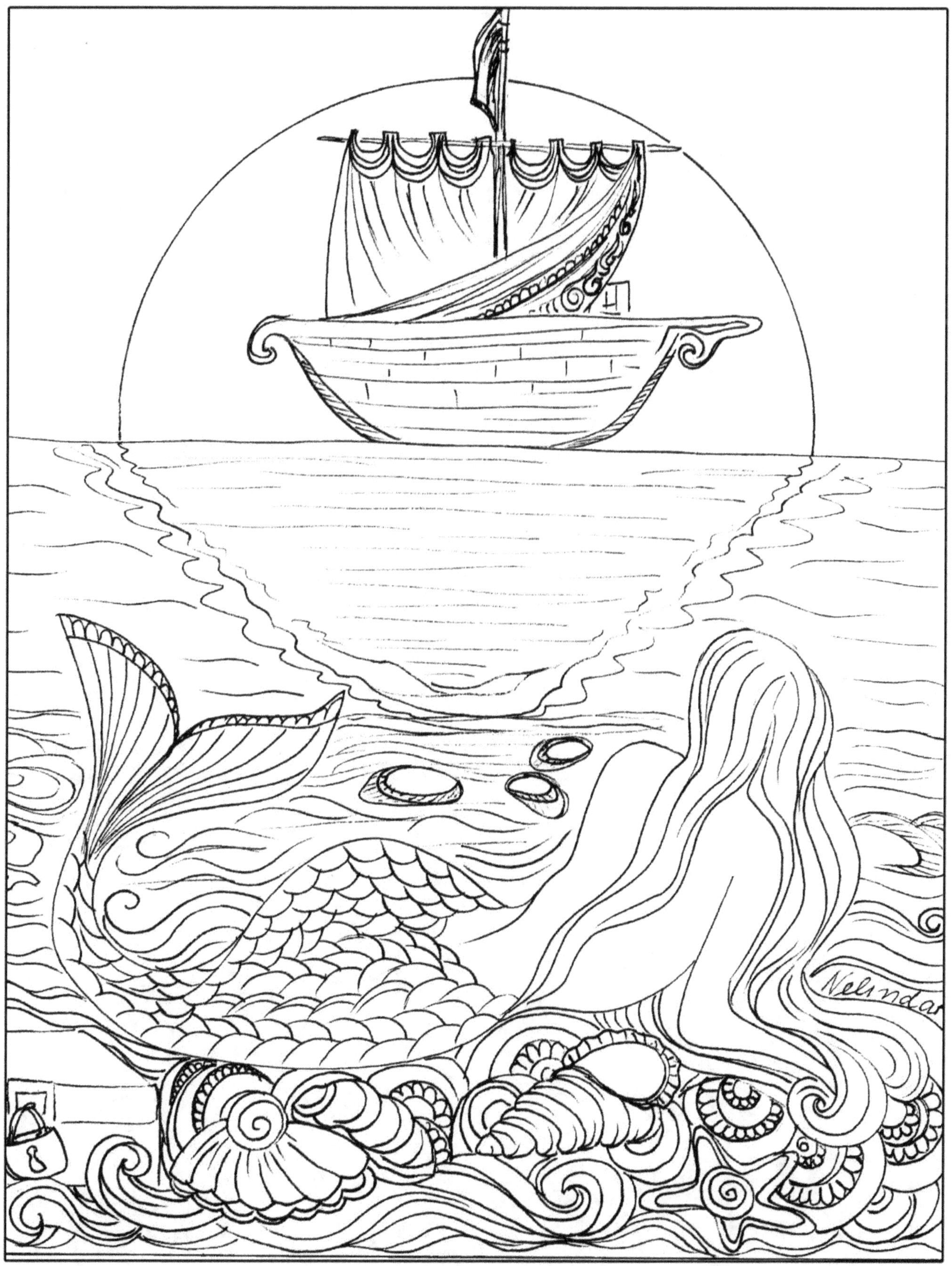

Syrenka Warszawska (Warsaw Mermaid) – Poland. Fish escaping from a fisherman's net means their local mermaid is to blame. Once they hear her beautiful songs, they decide not to punish her.

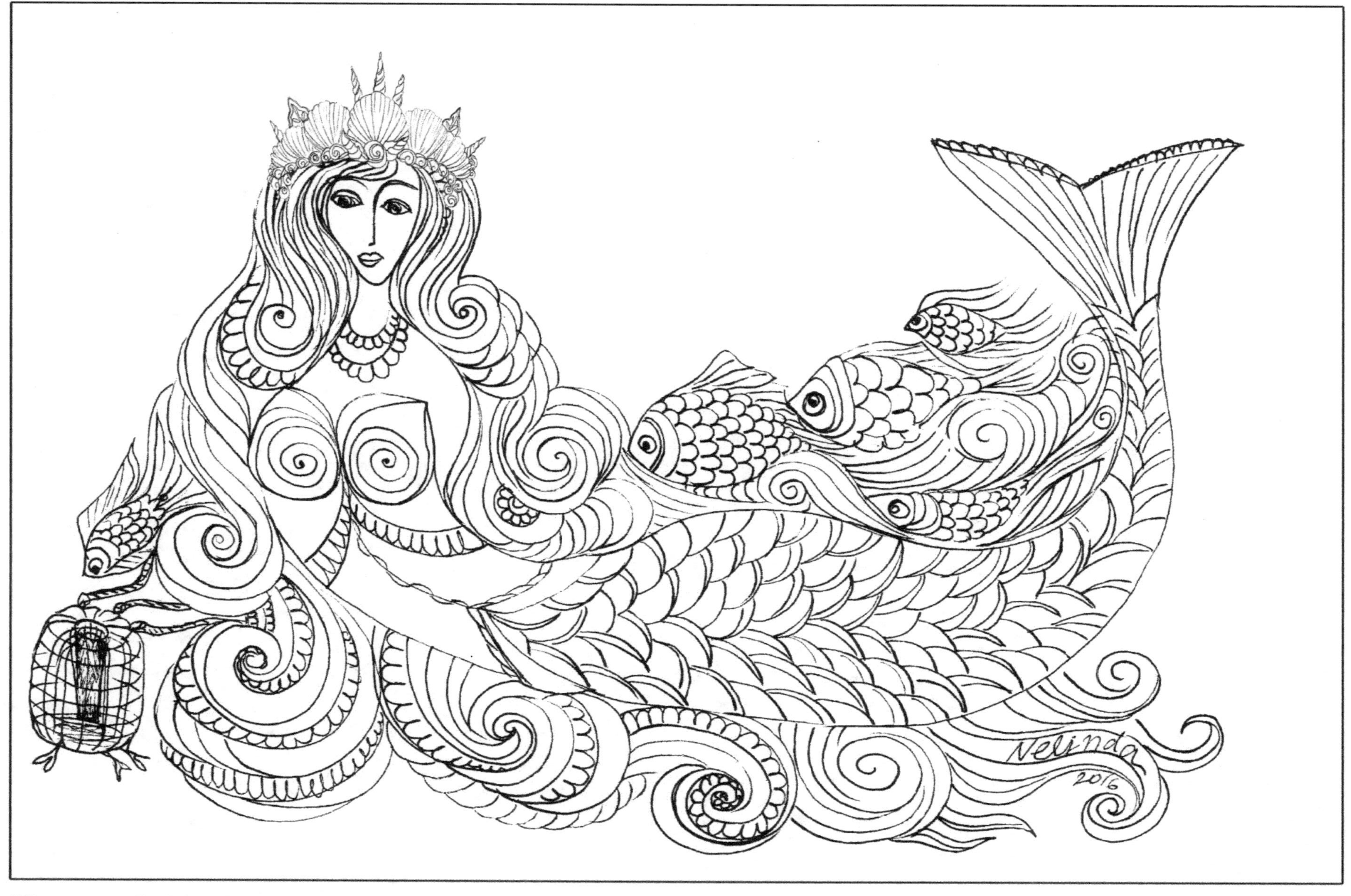

Merrows – Ireland. Mermaids lured humans into the water by promising friendship. Instead, they trapped their souls in a magical cage. Only the maker of the cage could unlock the spell.

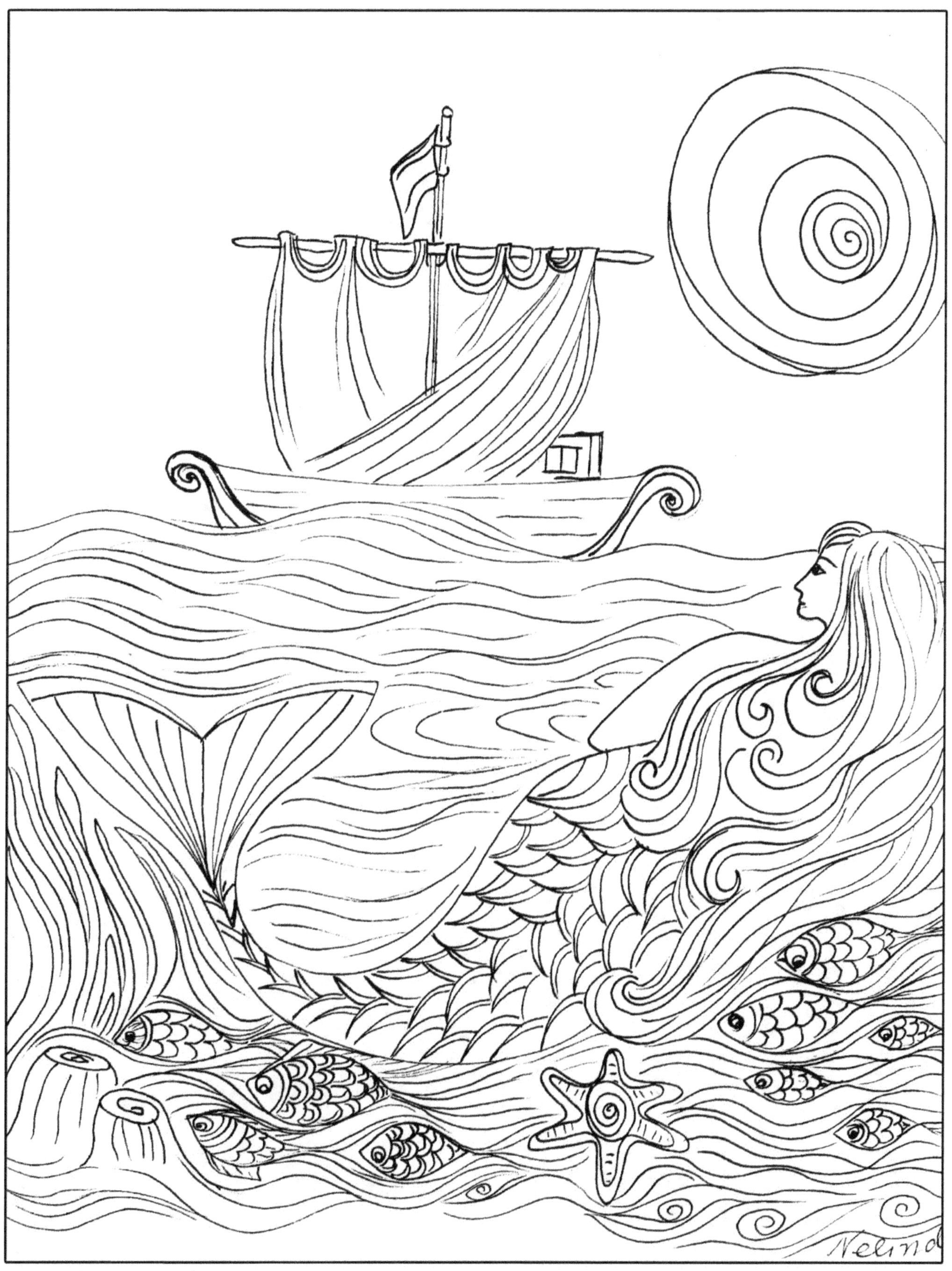

Nyai Loro Kidul – Indonesia. Forced to choose between his wife and daughter, a king forces a witch to make his daughter suffer a skin disease so she'll be banished. The girl dives into the sea and is cured.

www.ronesaavela.com

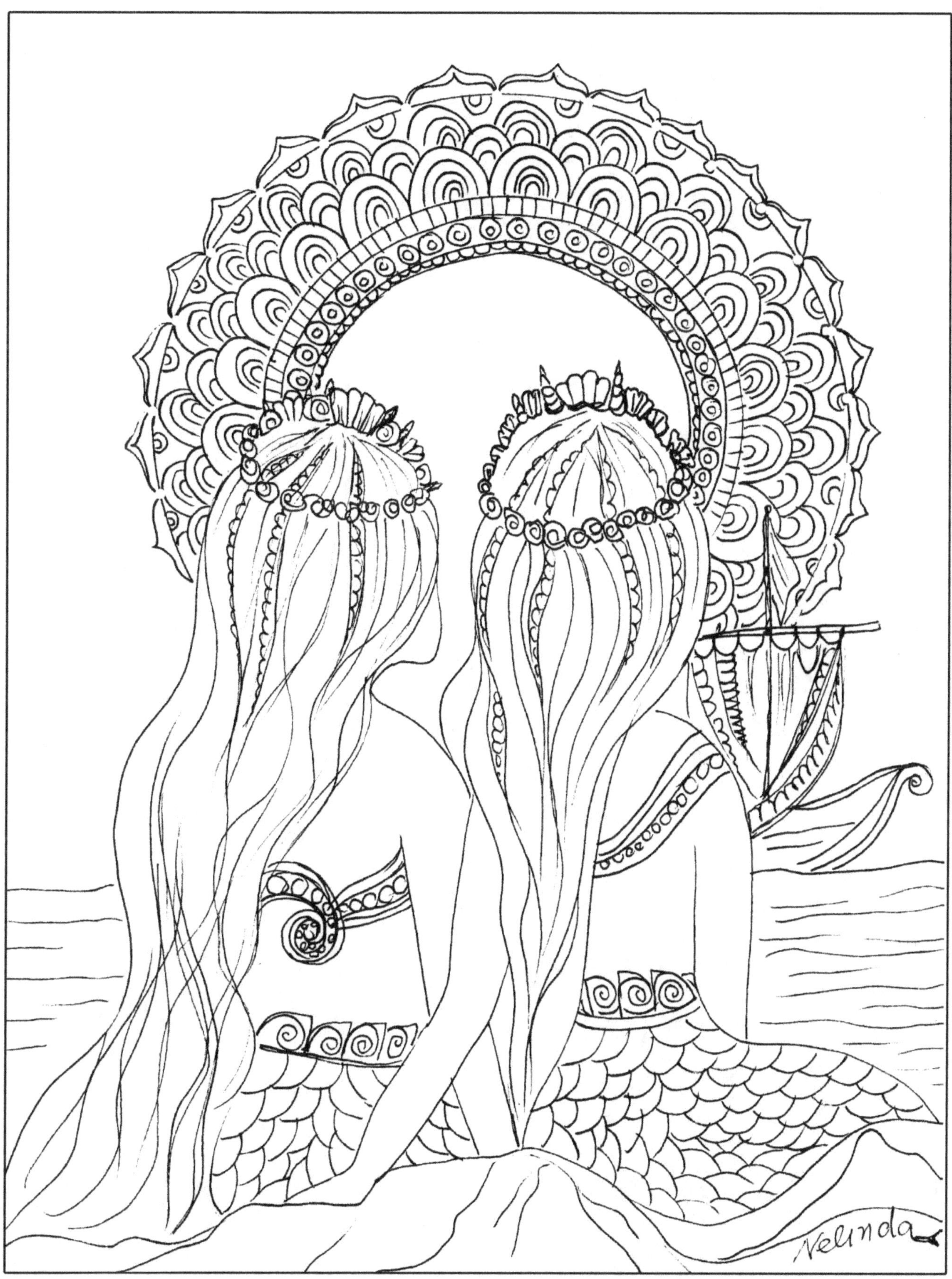

Ne Hwas – Native American (Passamaquoddy). Two girls disobey their parents and swim in enchanted waters, only to transform into mermaids and forever have to tow their parent's canoe.

www.ronesaaveela.com

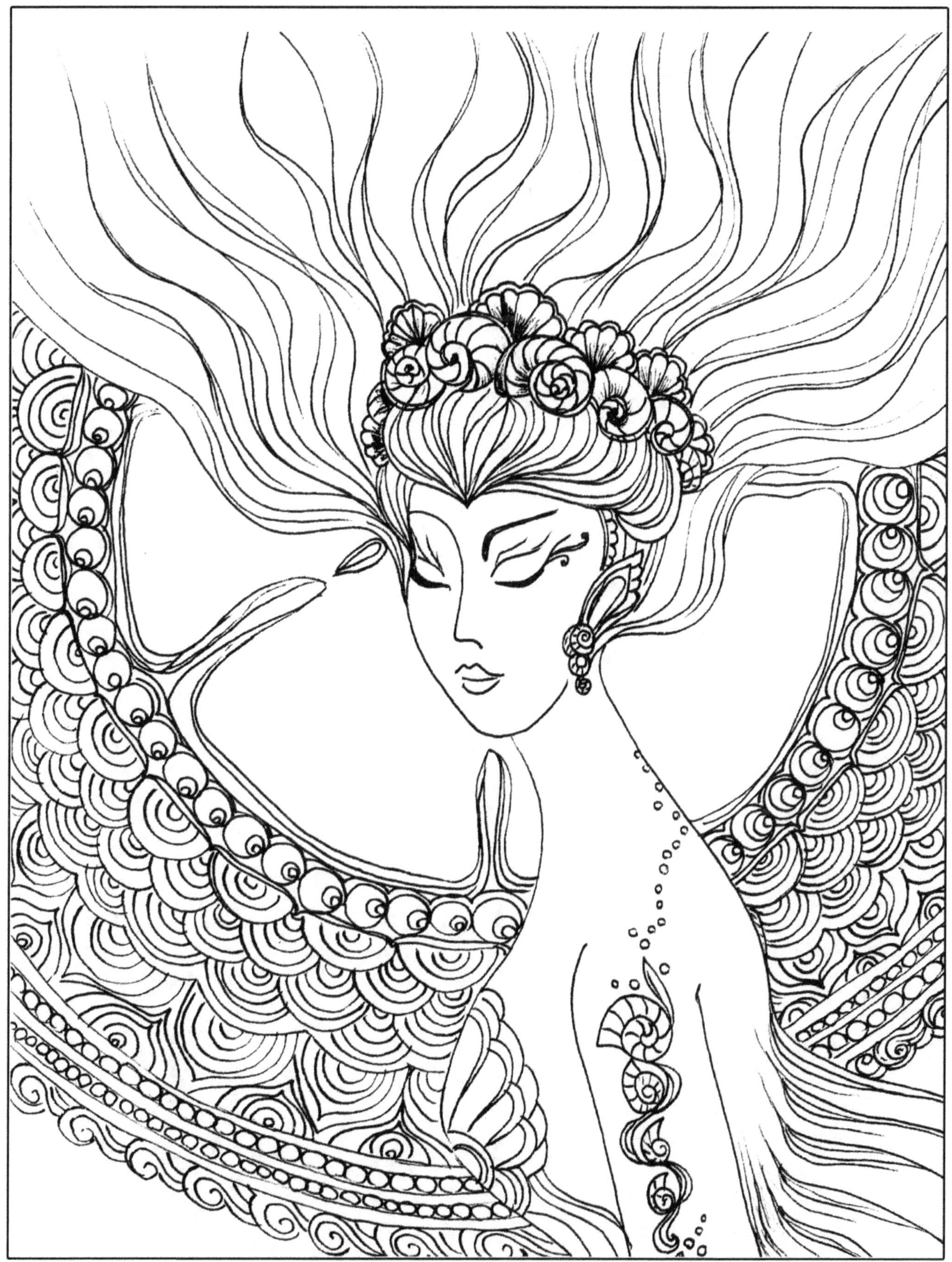

Ningyo – Japan. If a sailor caught a Ningyo, he would throw it back into the sea to avoid the creature causing a storm and misfortune.

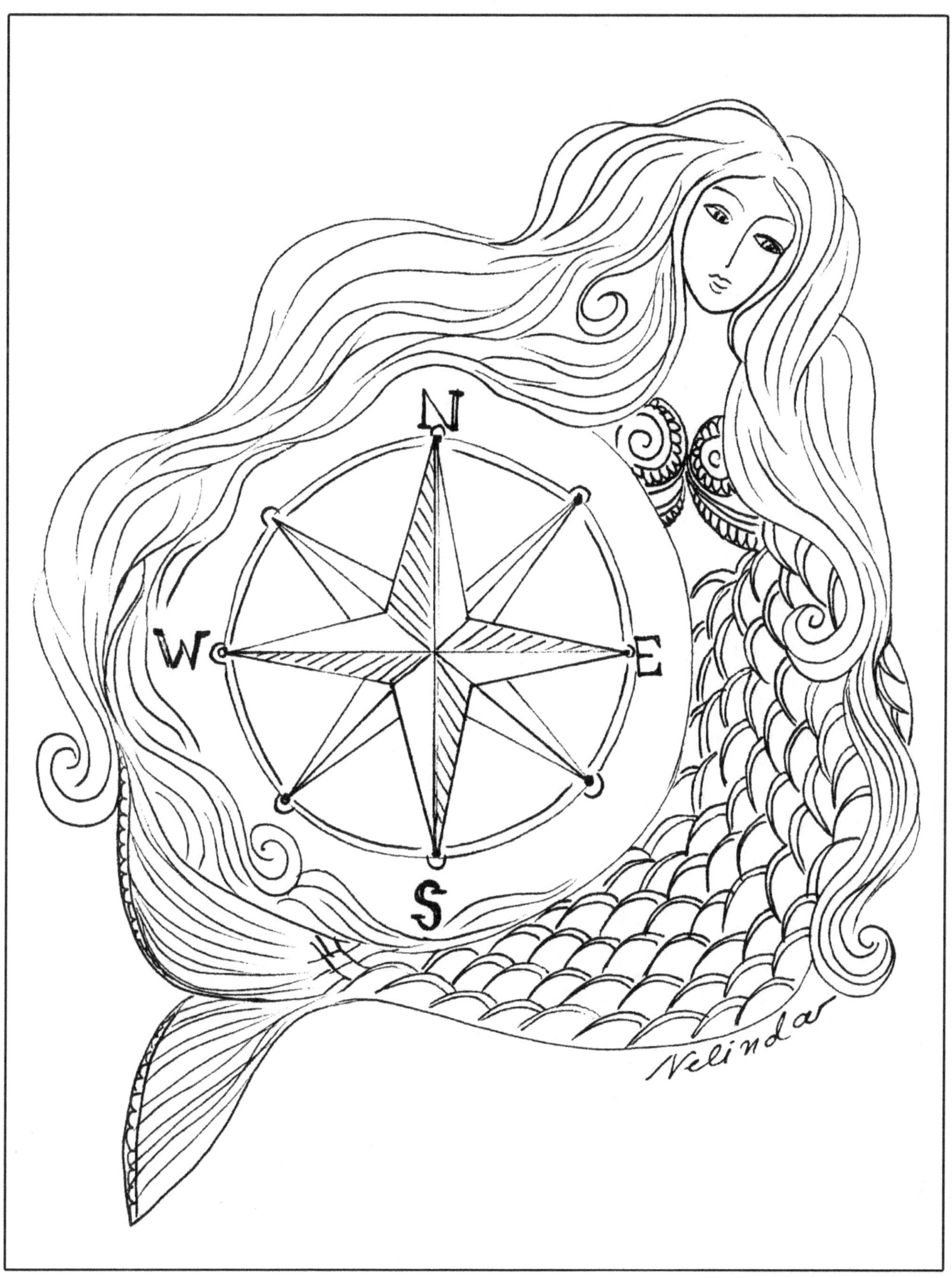

Thessalonike – Macedonia. For centuries, the sister of Alexander the Great asks sailors passing in the Agean if King Alexander lives. They always reply, "He lives and reigns and conquers the world."

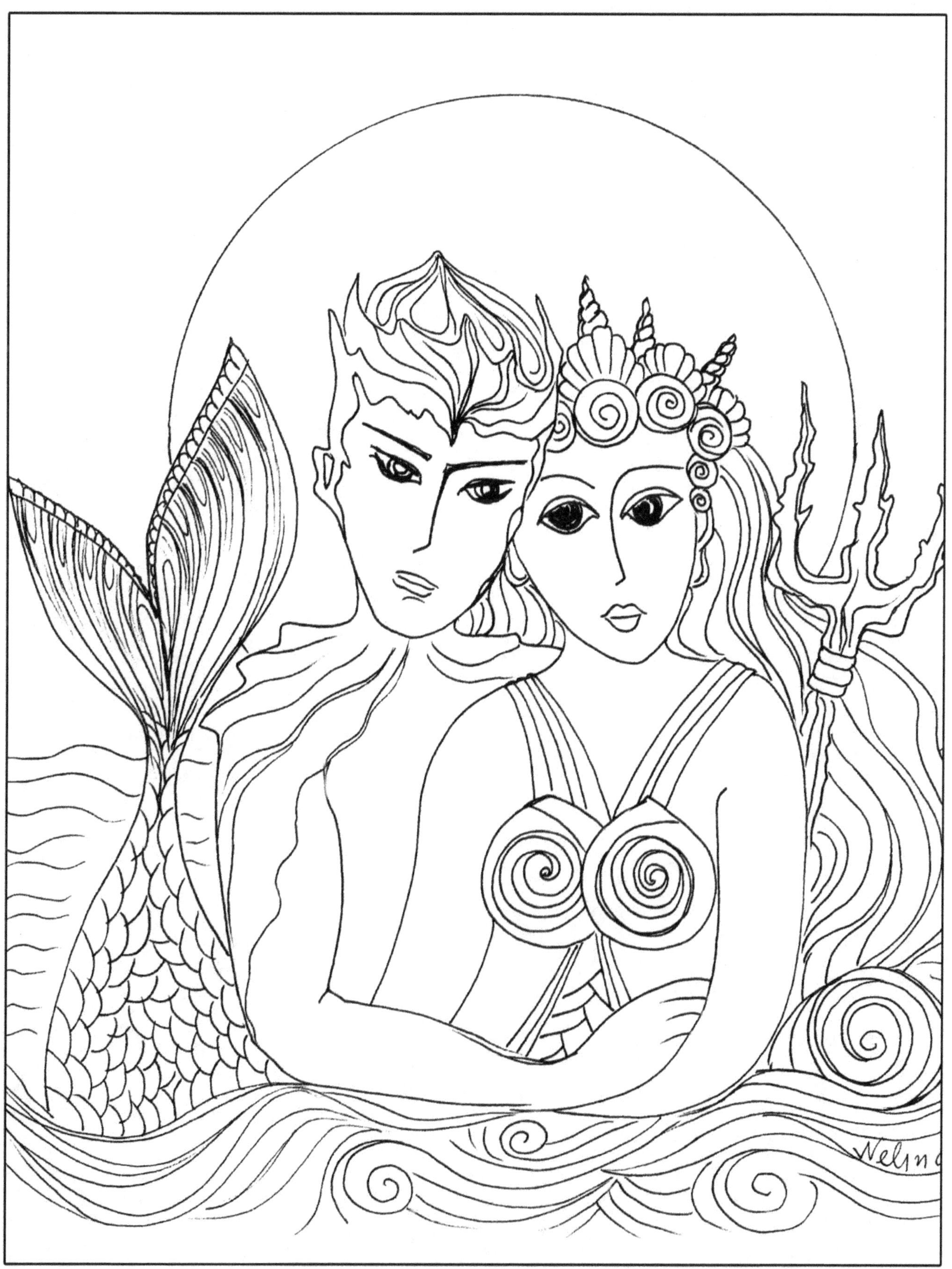

The Fish Husband – Nigeria. When a girl's parents discovered she married a fish man, her father sends her away and kills the husband. Brokenhearted, the girl jumps into the water and becomes an *onijegi* (mermaid).

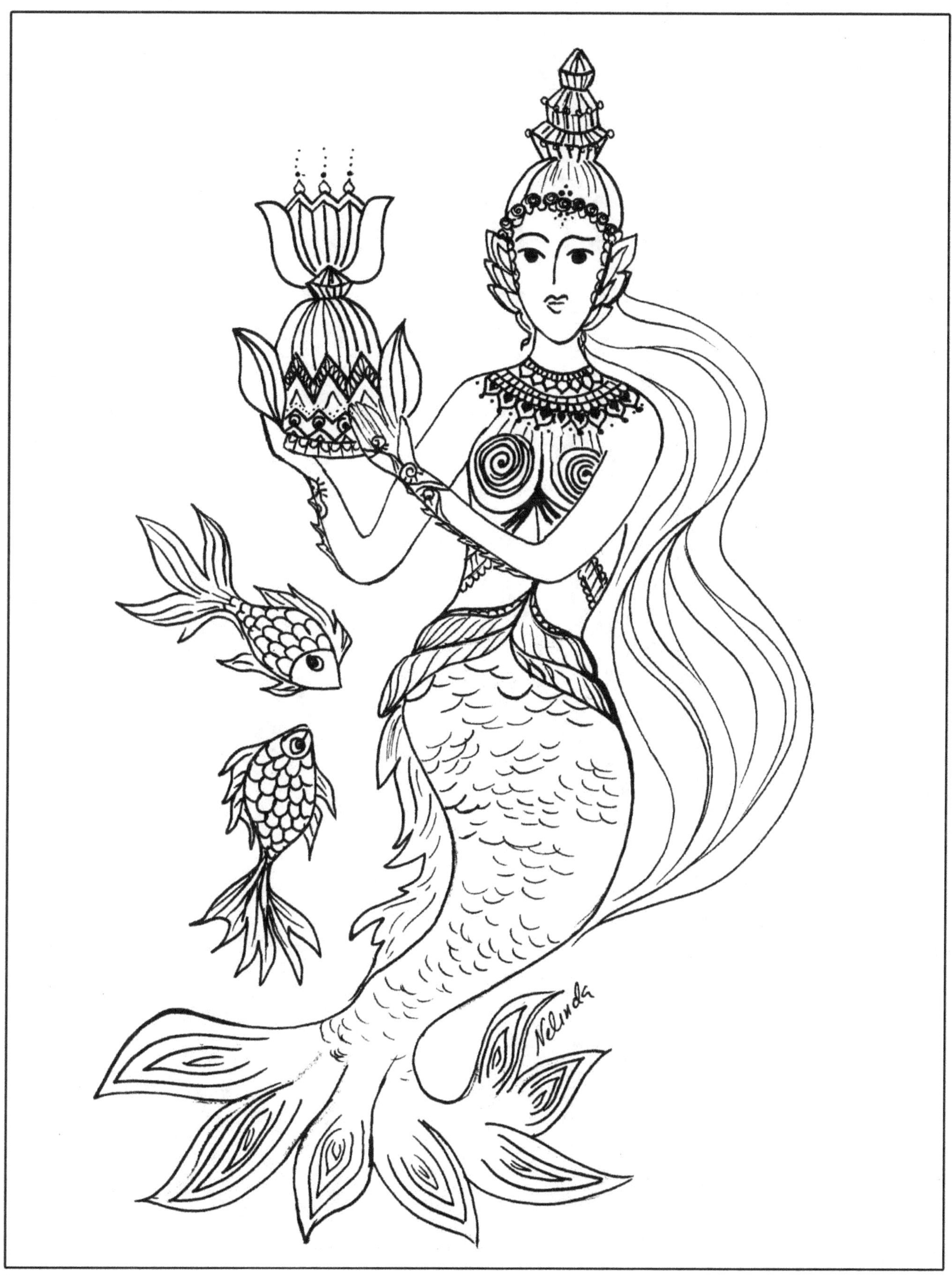

Suvannamaccha – Thailand. Mermaids carried away rocks that men threw into a river in order to build a bridge to rescue a woman captured by a demon. Hanuman attempted to capture the lead mermaid, only to fall in love with her.

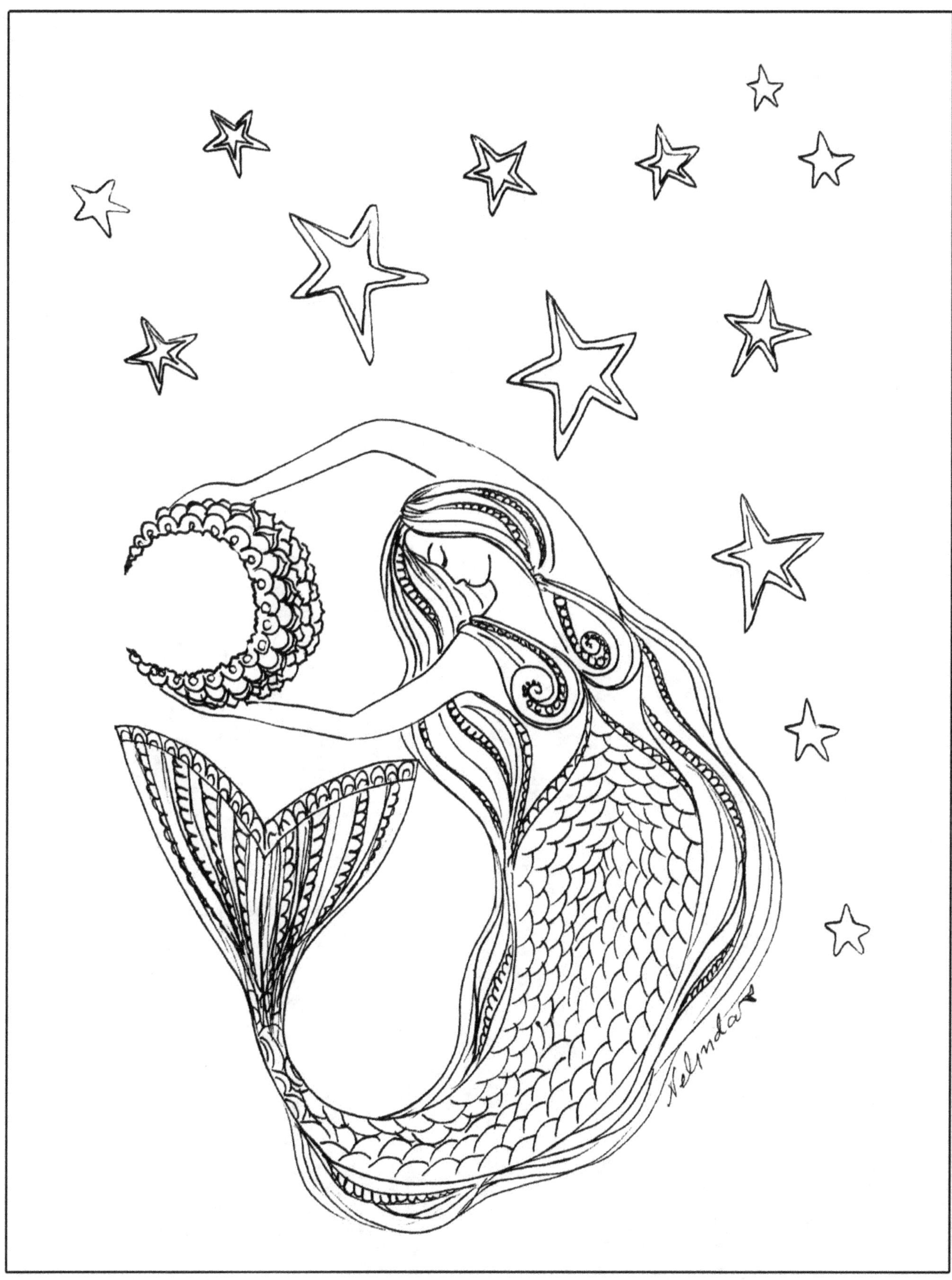

Mermaids are known for luring sailors to their death, but they can also be kind. If you do a favor for a mermaid, she will be grateful and give you a magical gift.

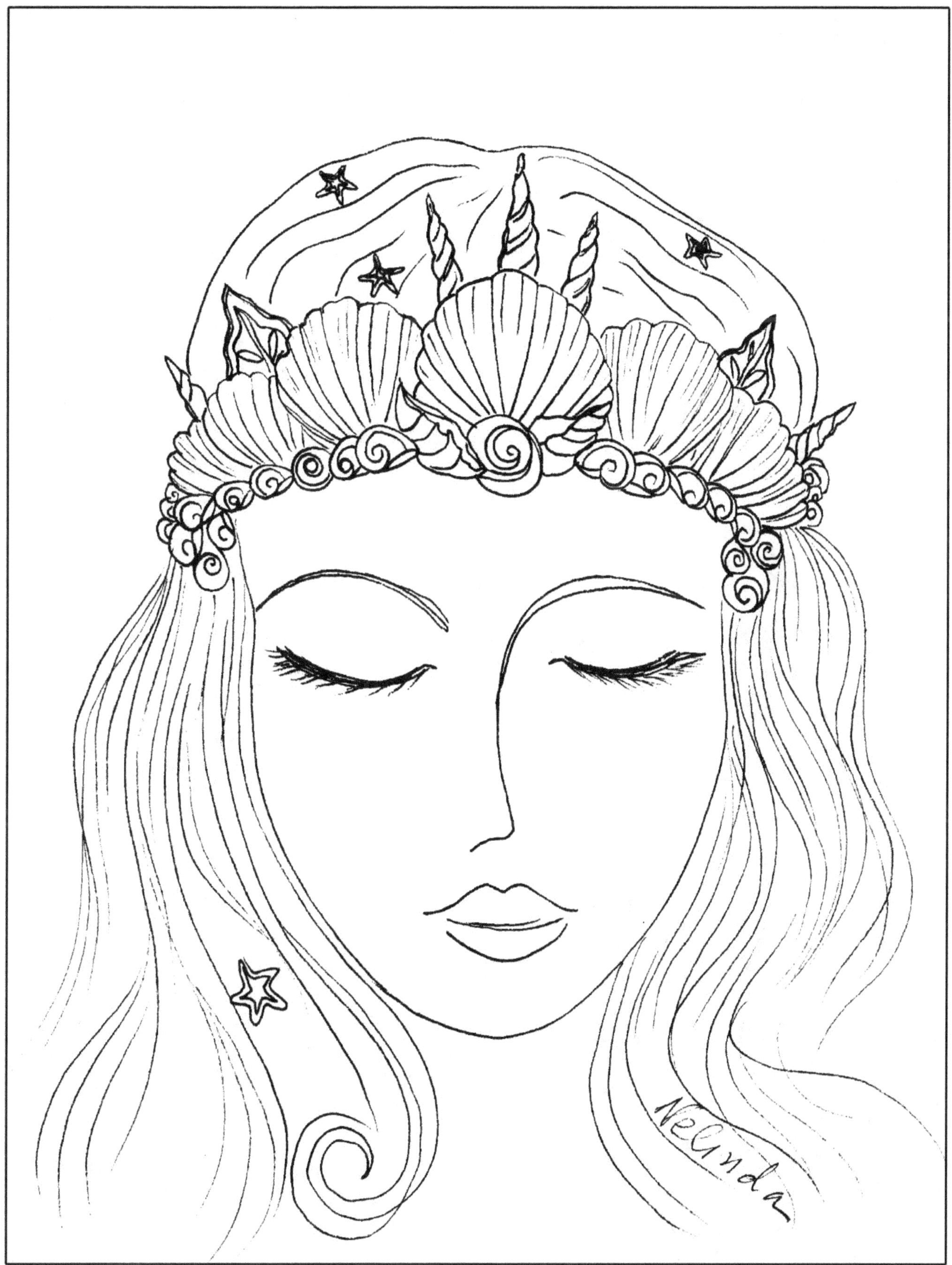

Aquamarine is the gemstone of the sea, which mermaids cherish. People once believed it was a mermaid's tears and had the power to protect sailors at sea.

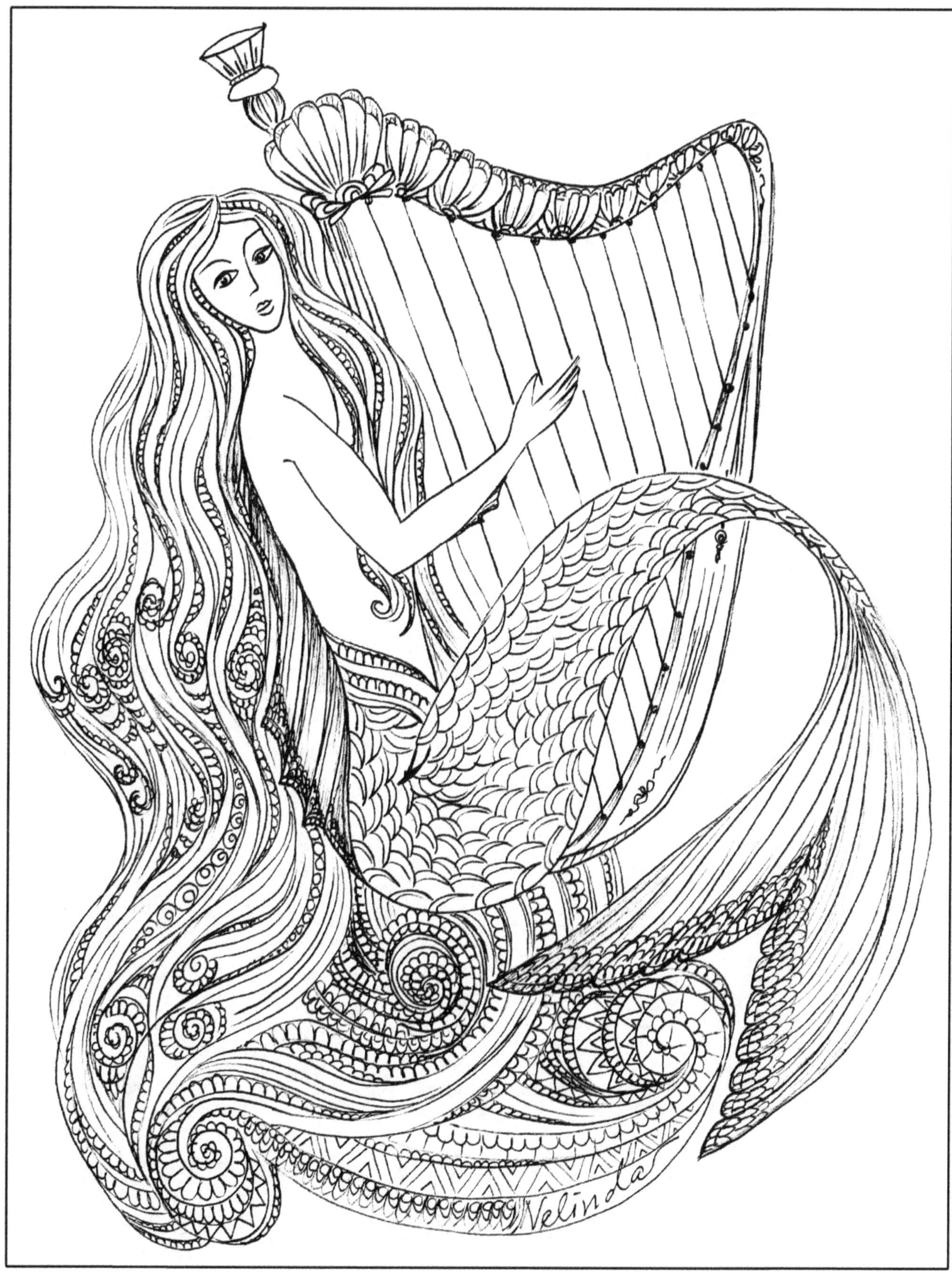

Lorelei – Germany. Atop cliffs, the lorelei lured sailors to their death with their beautiful songs. From poem, Die Lorelei, by Heinrich Heine: "But a gold harp from her feet / Lifted she ere long, / And its music, pulsing sweet, / Fed a wondrous song."

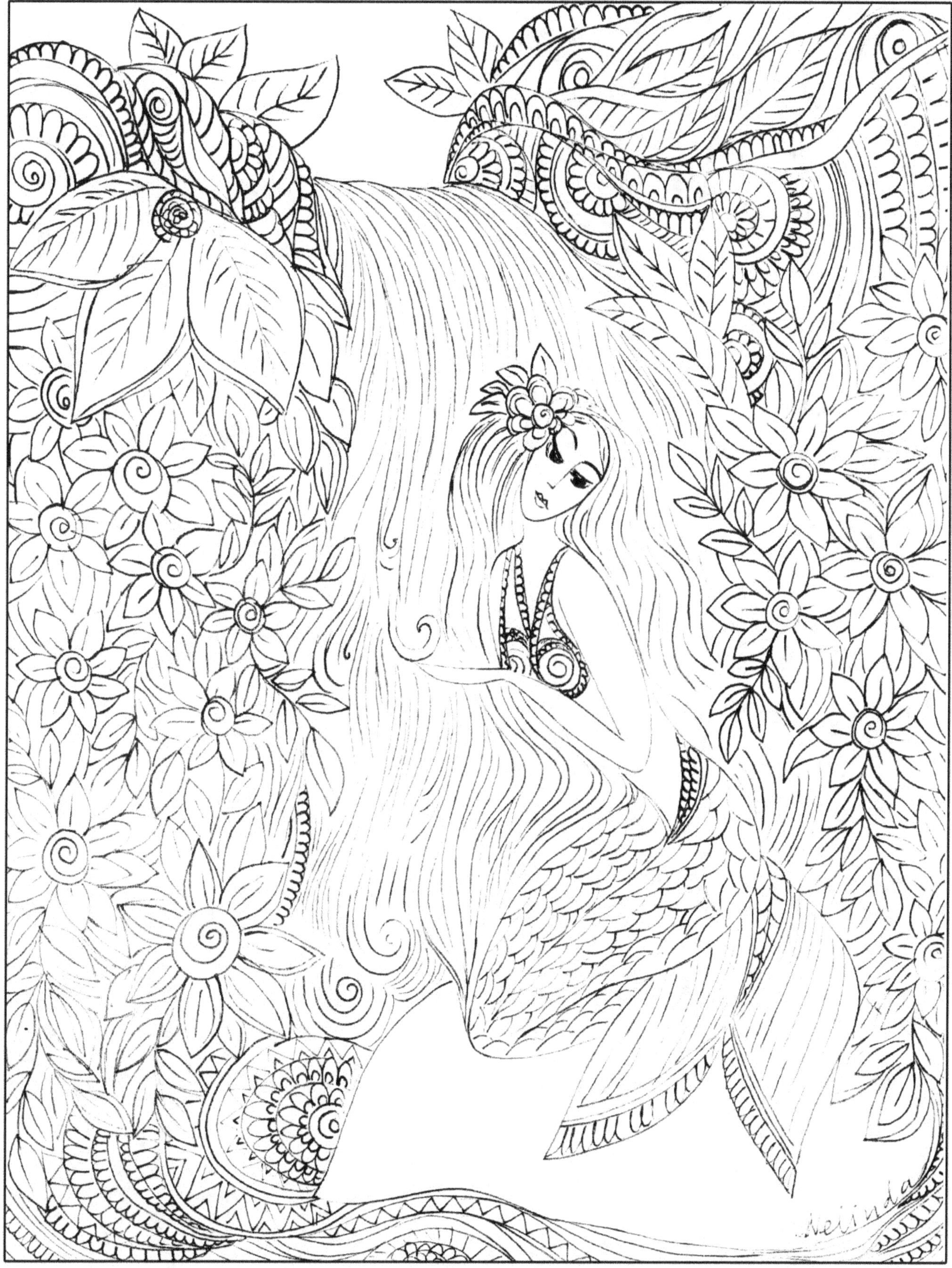

Undine – Ancient Greece. Found in forest pools and waterfalls, undines had tragic lives. Human husbands were always unfaithful, and therefore fated to die.

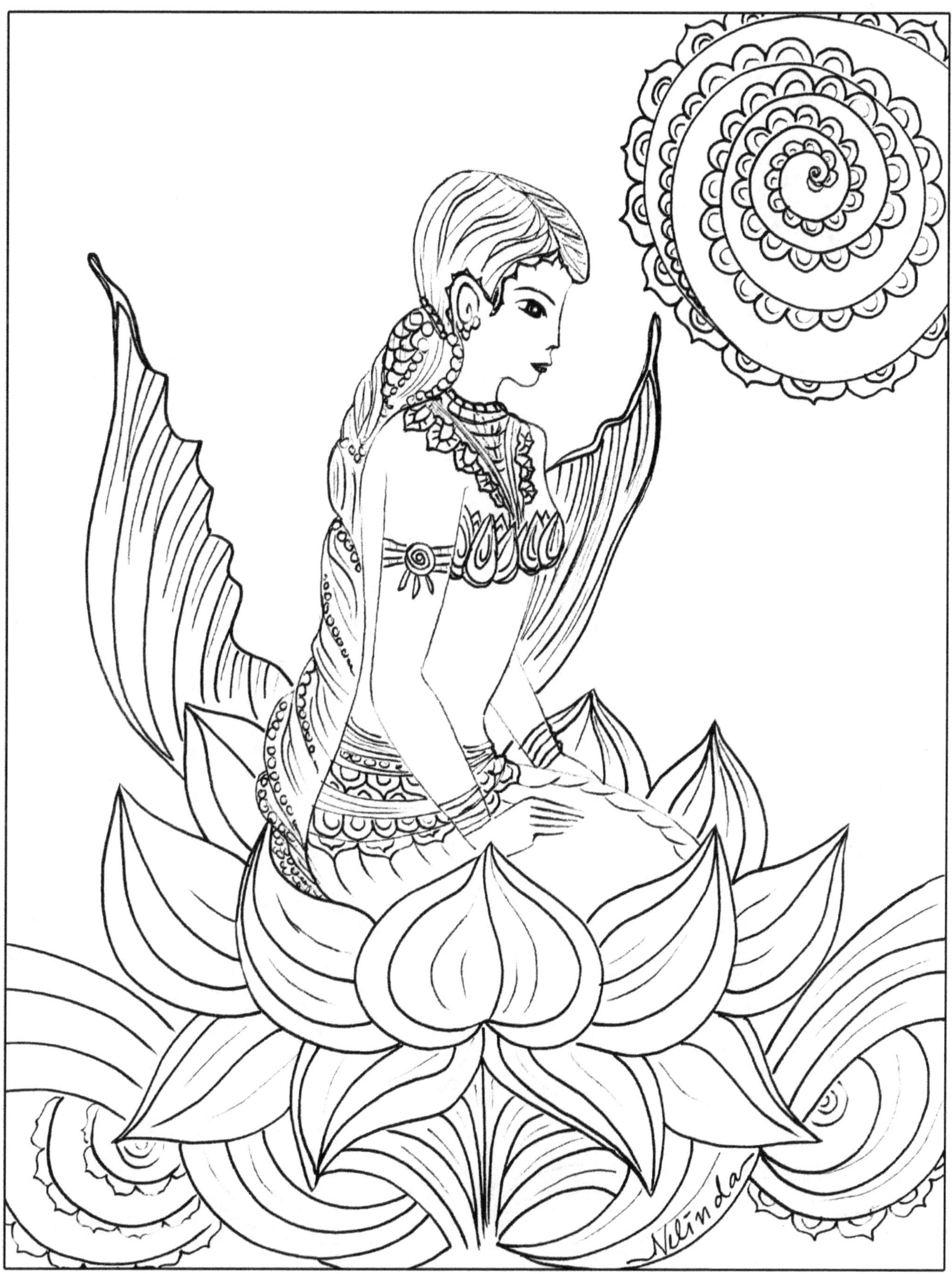

Apsaras – Hindu. These water and cloud spirits are shape-shifters who come down from Indra (heaven) to seduce men with their dance.

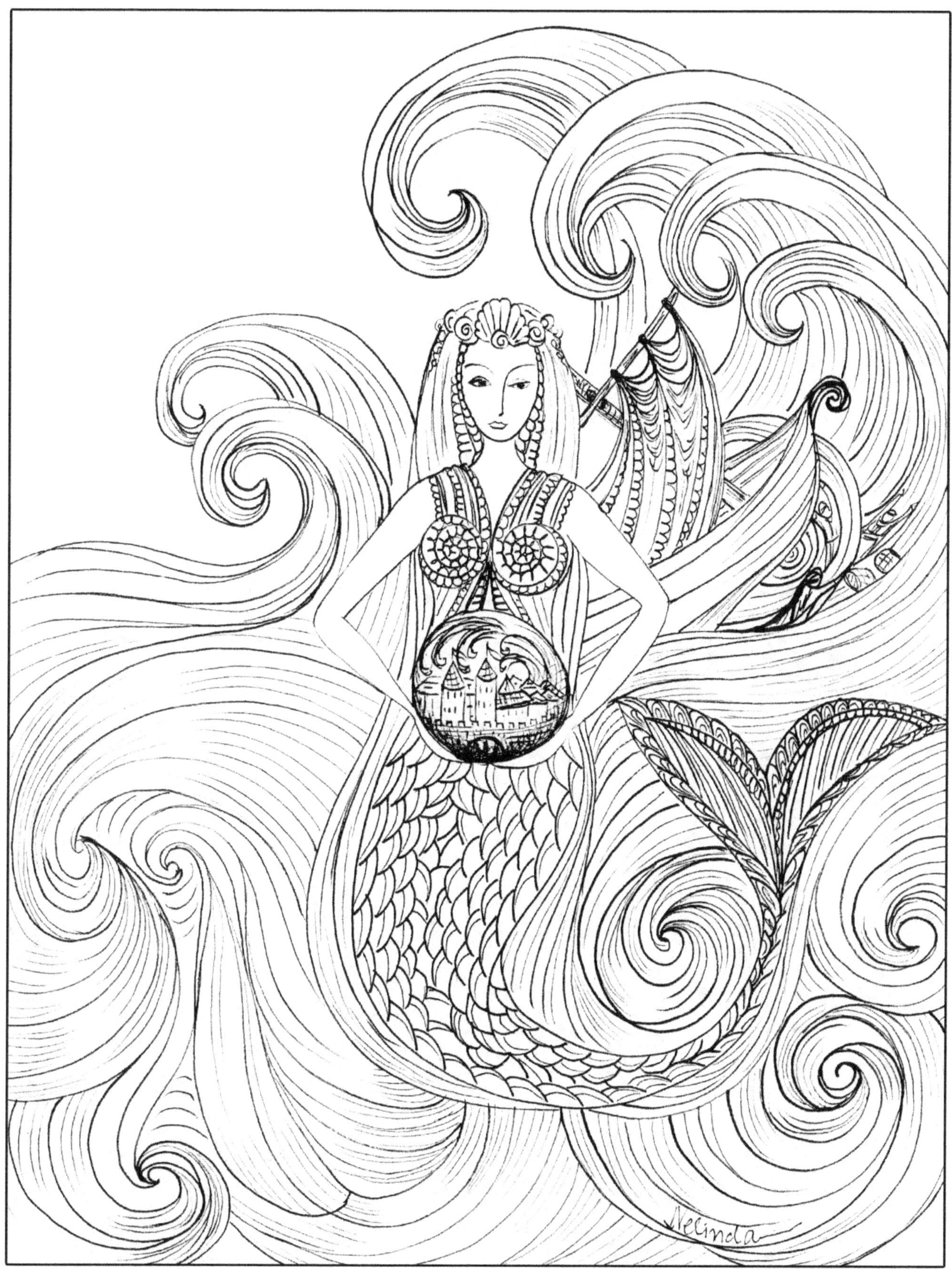

Morgen – Welsh. While drunk, Dahut, a king's daughter, opened the city gates during a storm. A tidal wave covered the city. Dahut and her father escaped on a magical flying horse, but the king pushed his evil daughter off into the sea, where she became a morgen.

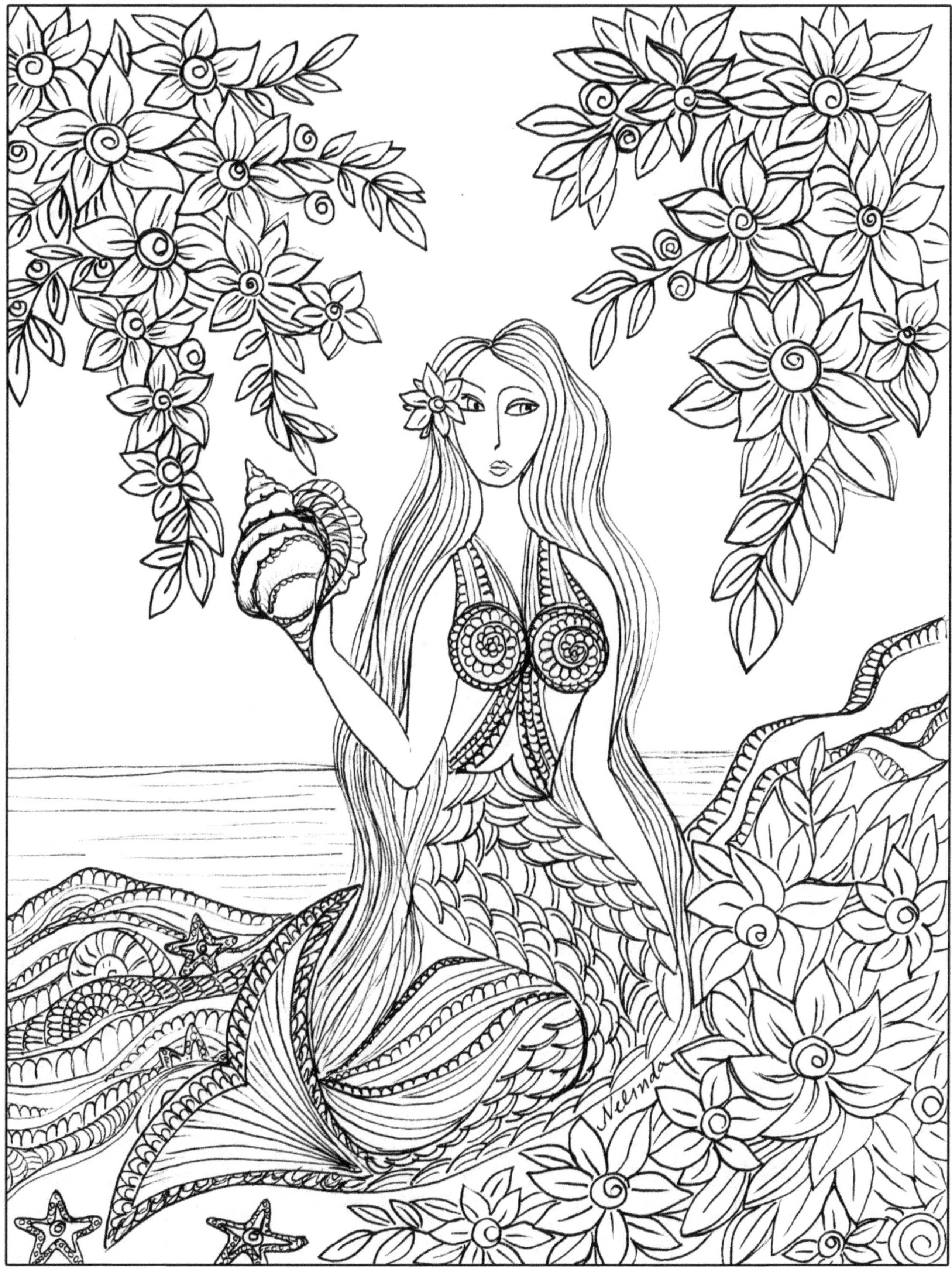

Aycayia - Caribbean. Meaning "she with a lovely voice," this seductive woman was sent out to sea to keep her away from men. Some say she was turned into a red flower, which brides wear, reminding the groom not to pay attention to other women.

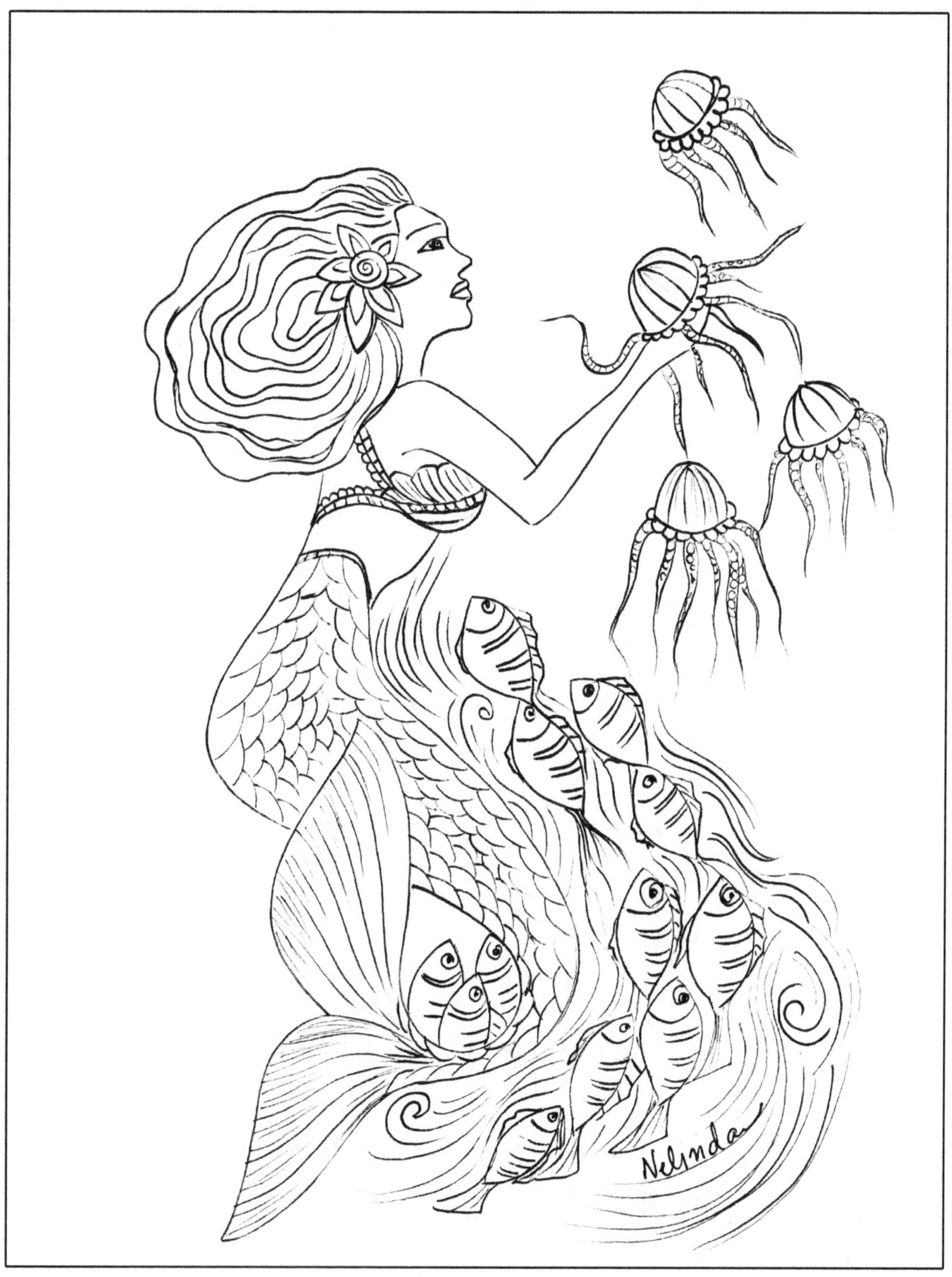

Meingu – Cameroon. Creatures of rivers and seas, these mermaids bring good fortune to, and cure diseases of, people who worship them. They are mediums between worshipers and the spirit world.

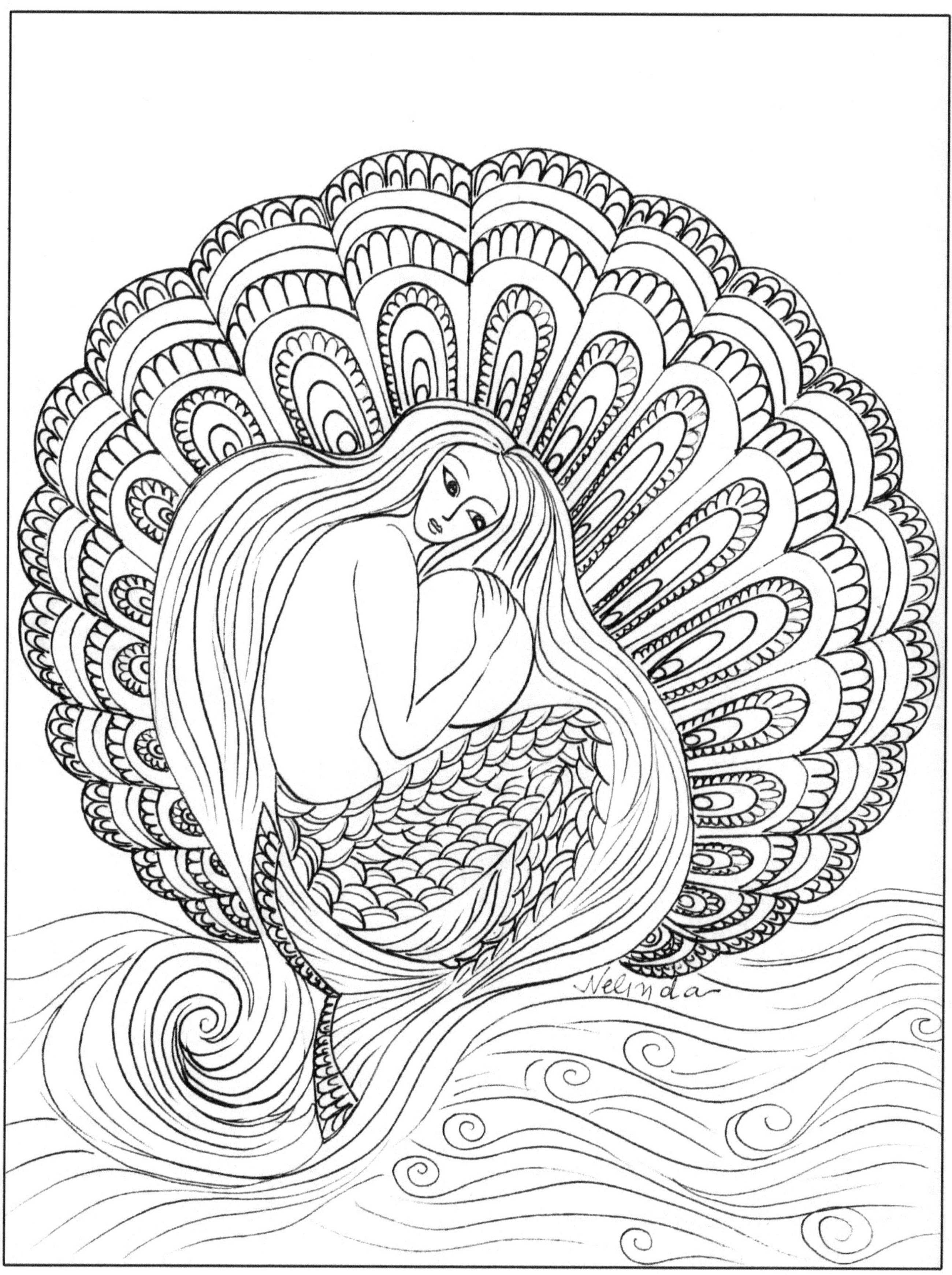

Jiāorén – China. A mermaid lived with a family and wove cloth called "Dragon Yarn" that never became wet, even in water. Before she returned to her home, she wept into a container and her tears became pearls.

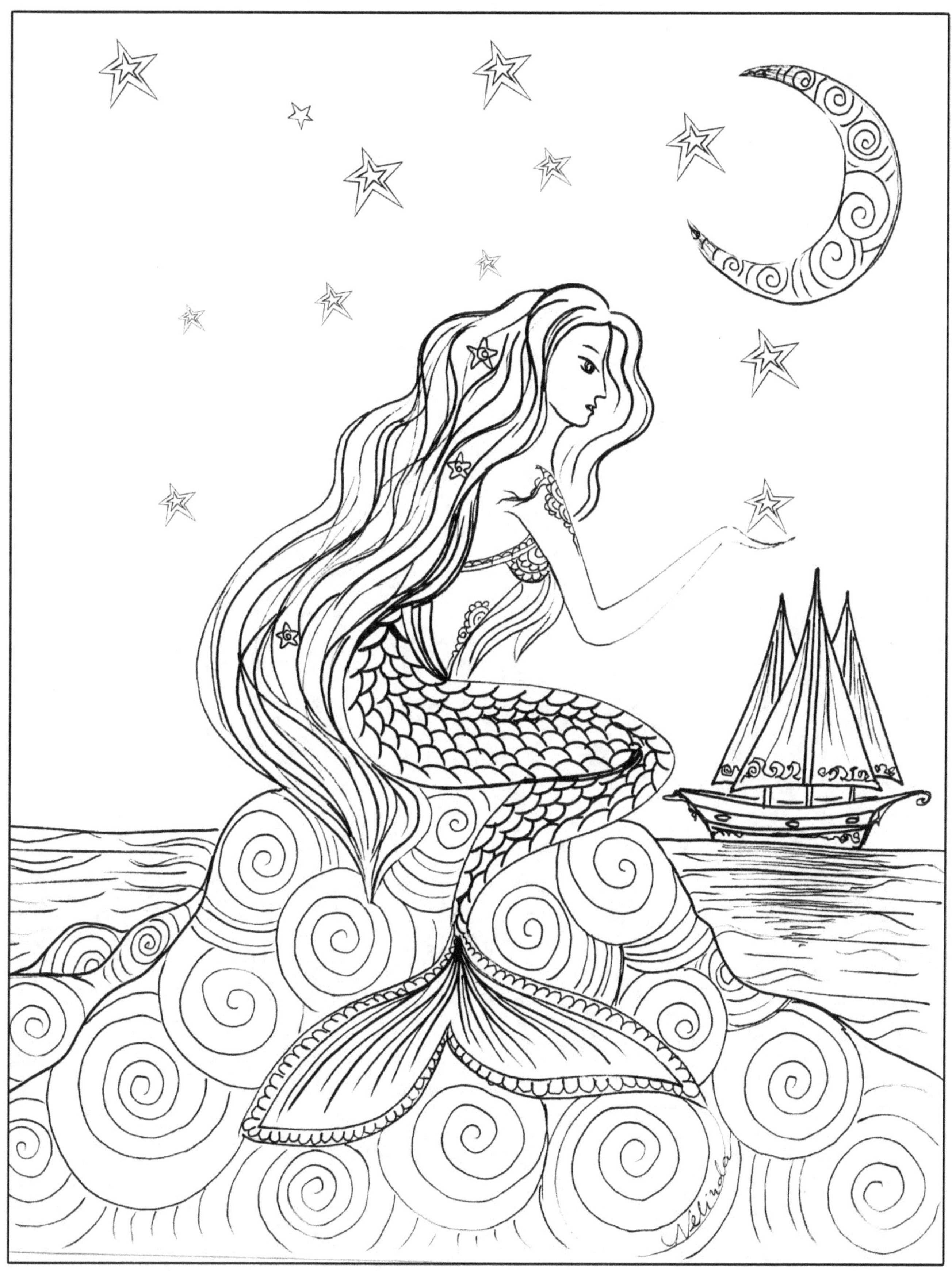

Mermaid of Iona – Scotland. A mermaid fell in love with a monk and prayed for a soul so she could marry him. Each night she shed tears that became green marble stones that protect the holder from drowning.

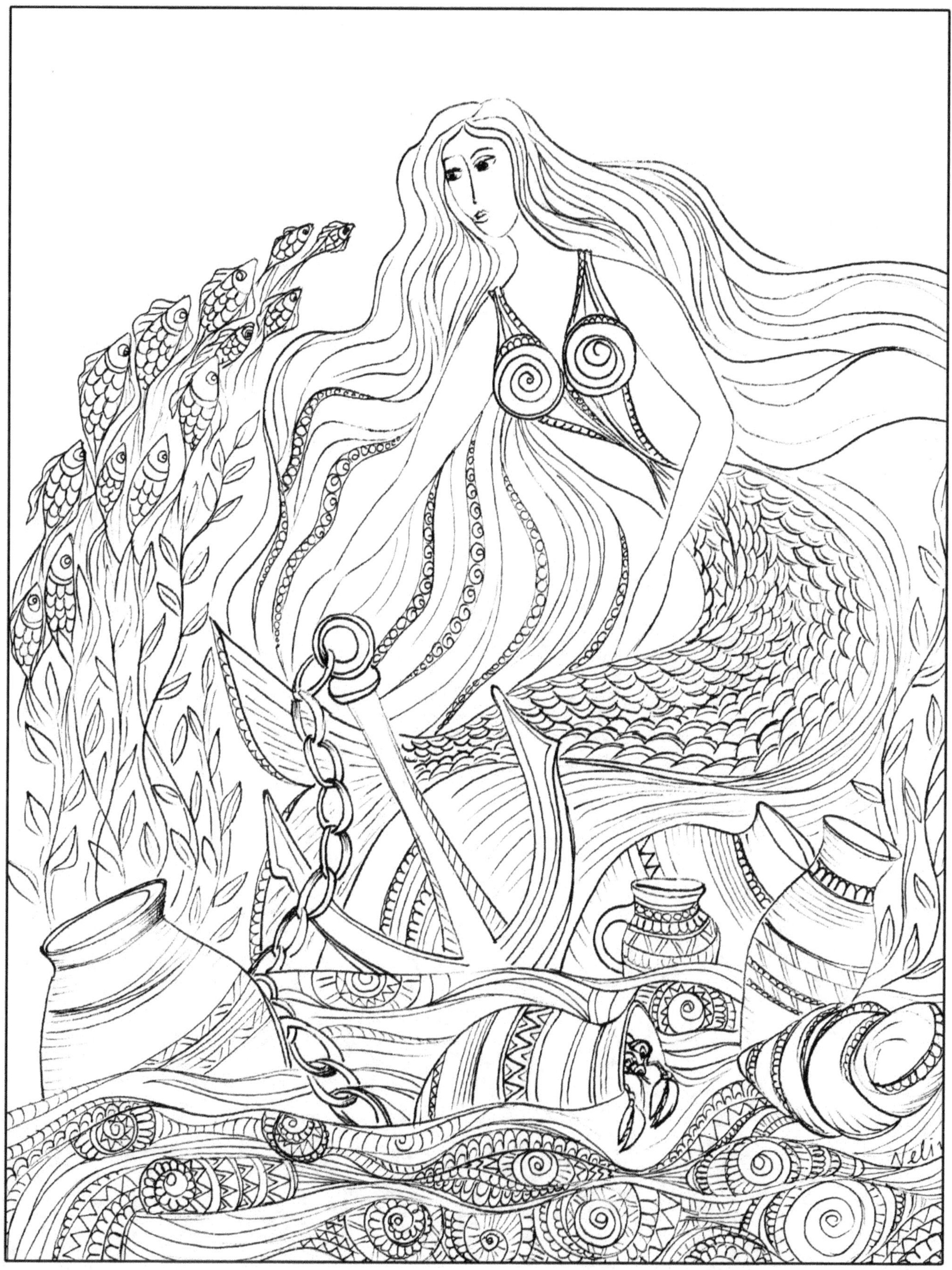

Bára – Norse. A Seer once fell in love with a mermaid, but seeing waves triggered his prophesies, so he couldn't visit her. She sang the storms into a shell, which she gave to her lover. Thereafter, anchors were created to help ground ships.

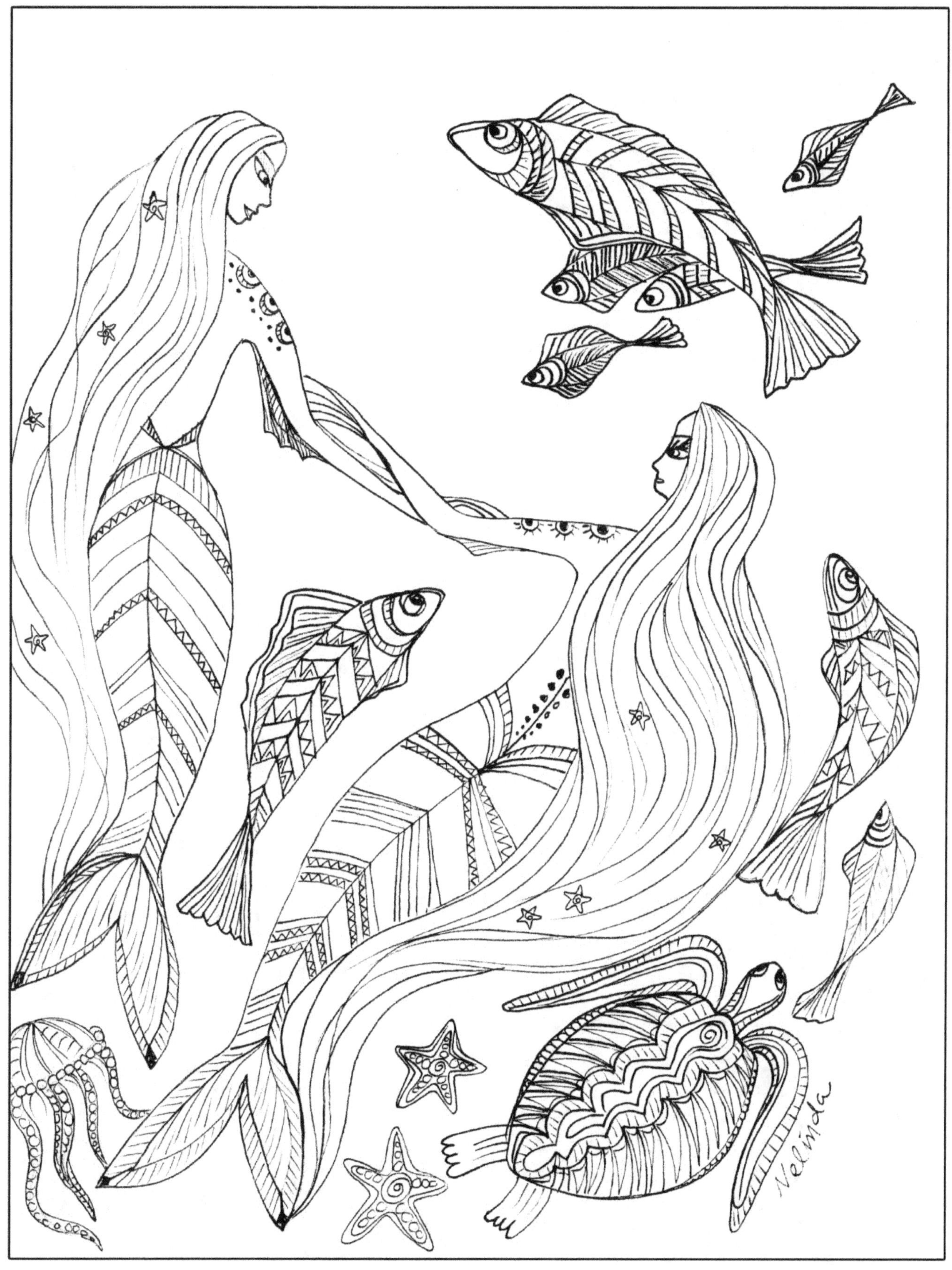

Yawkyawk – Australia. Found in streams and pools, these fertility mermaids are called the children of Ngalyod, the Rainbow Serpent. Going near their water hole can make a woman pregnant.

www.ronesaaveela.com

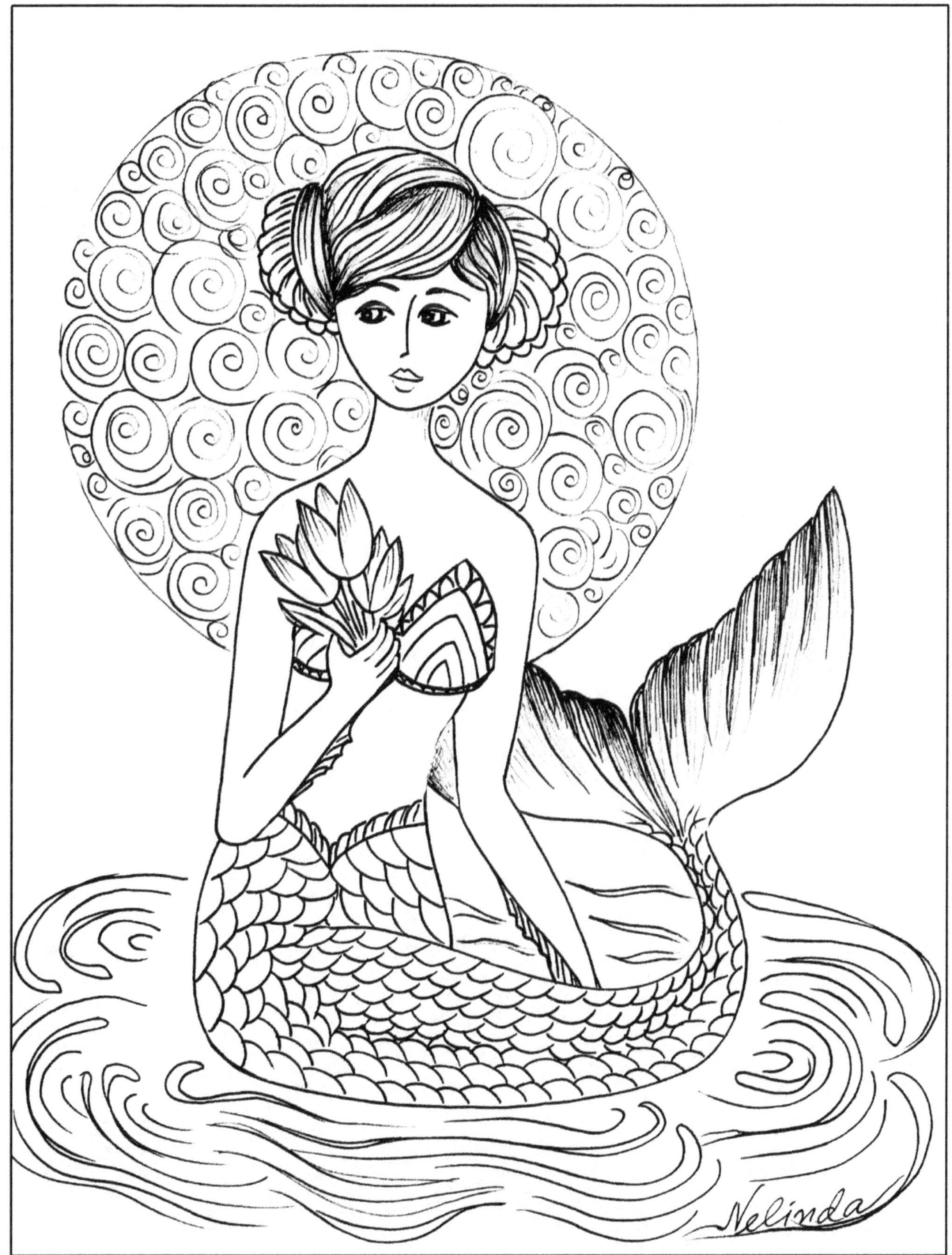

Edam Mermaid – Holland. In 1403, a mermaid was trapped in a lake after she swam through holes in the dike and couldn't find her way back to sea.

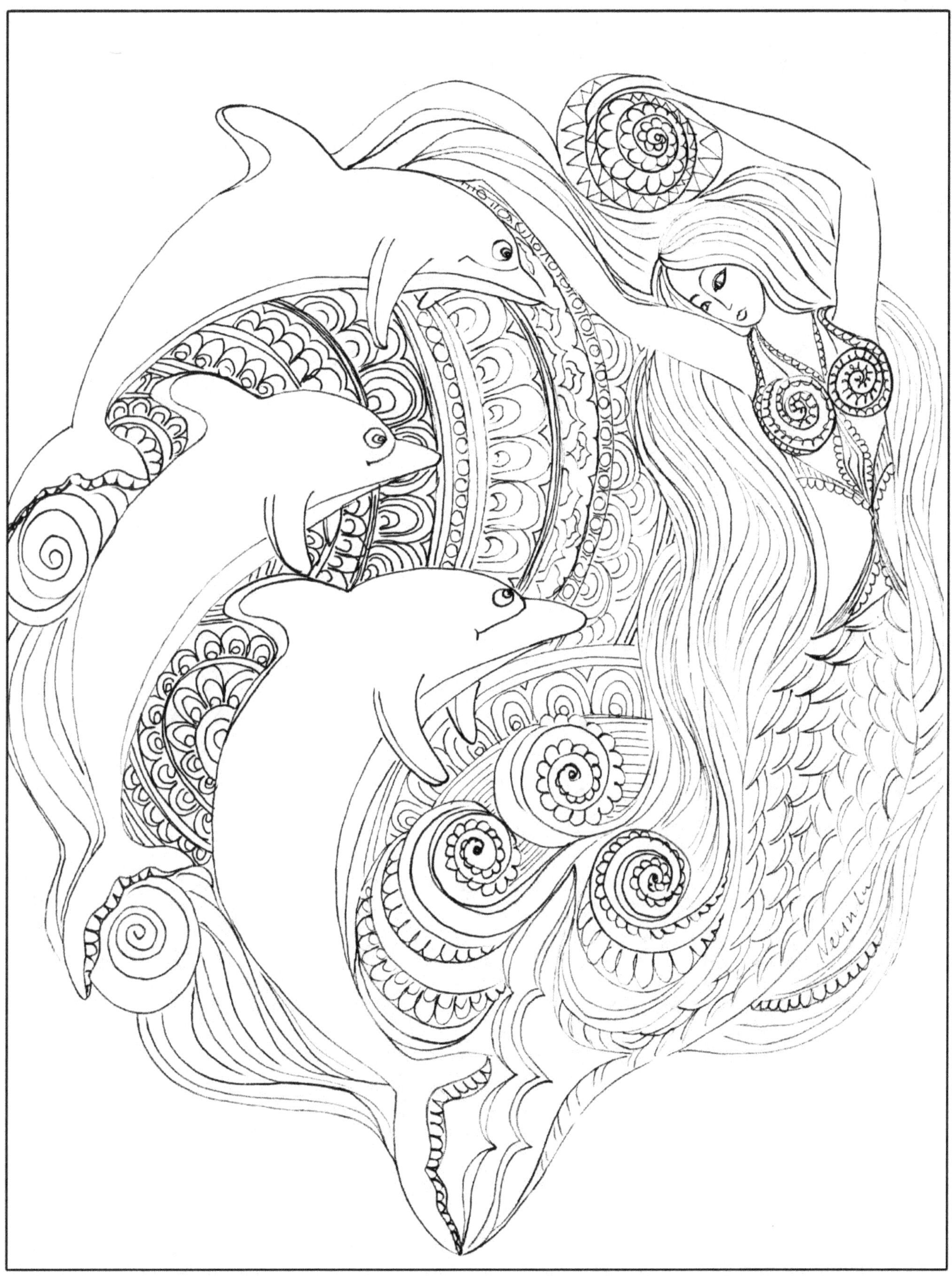

Dolphin Girl – Micronesia. A mermaid came to land and removed her tail to watch dances. A man hid her tail and she was forced to marry him and have his children. When she found her tail, she left, but not before warning her children never to eat dolphins.

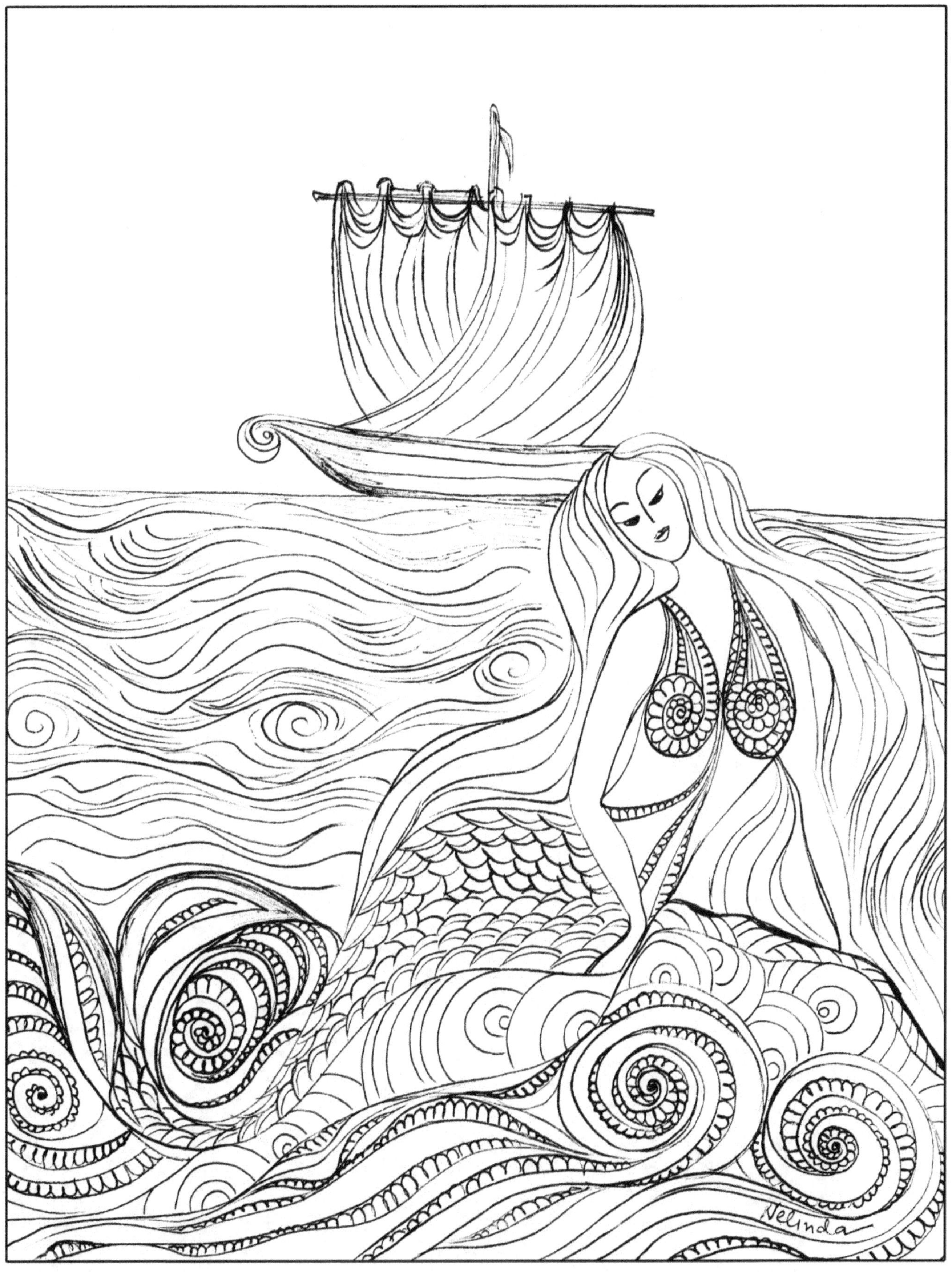

Yhtac – Argentina/Chile. A sorcerer named Arasmin flew around the world in his castle searching for this elusive mermaid, said to have golden scales.

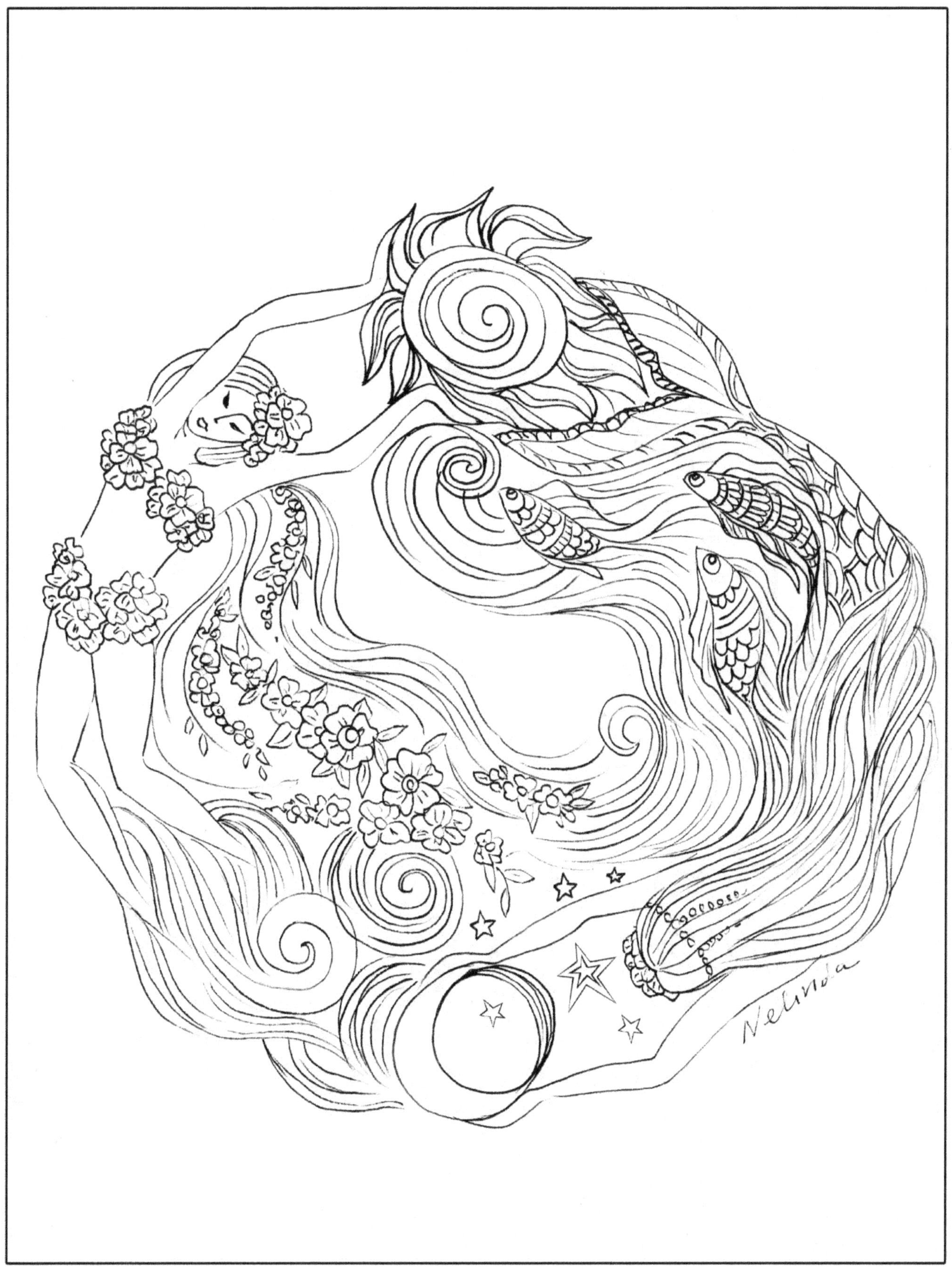

Iara – Brazil. After killing her brothers in self-defense, this warrior maiden was tossed into the river, where the River King gave her a tail in exchange for her legs.

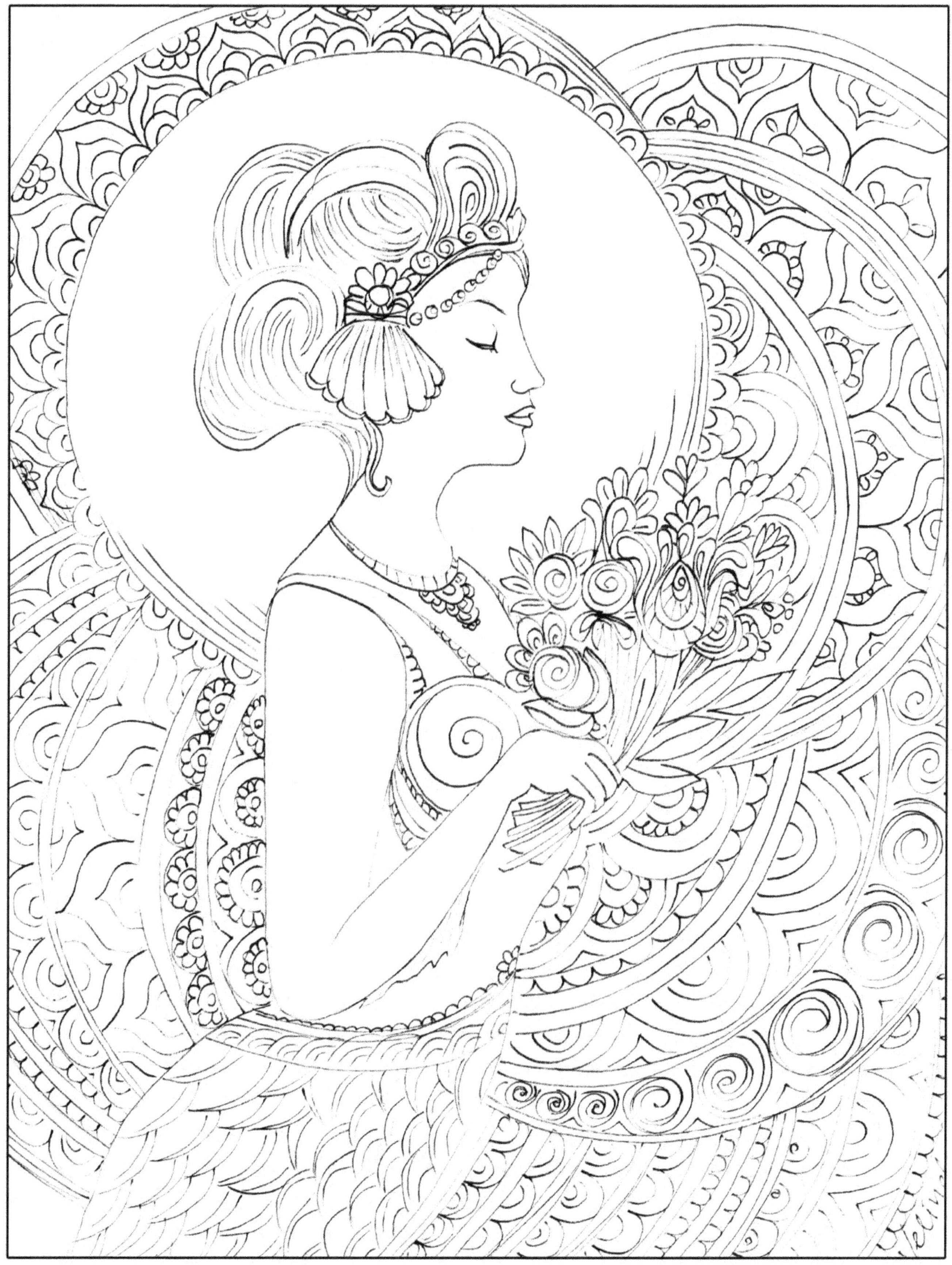

Nixe – Germany. These shape-shifting water spirits are often recognized in human form because the hem of their clothes is always wet.

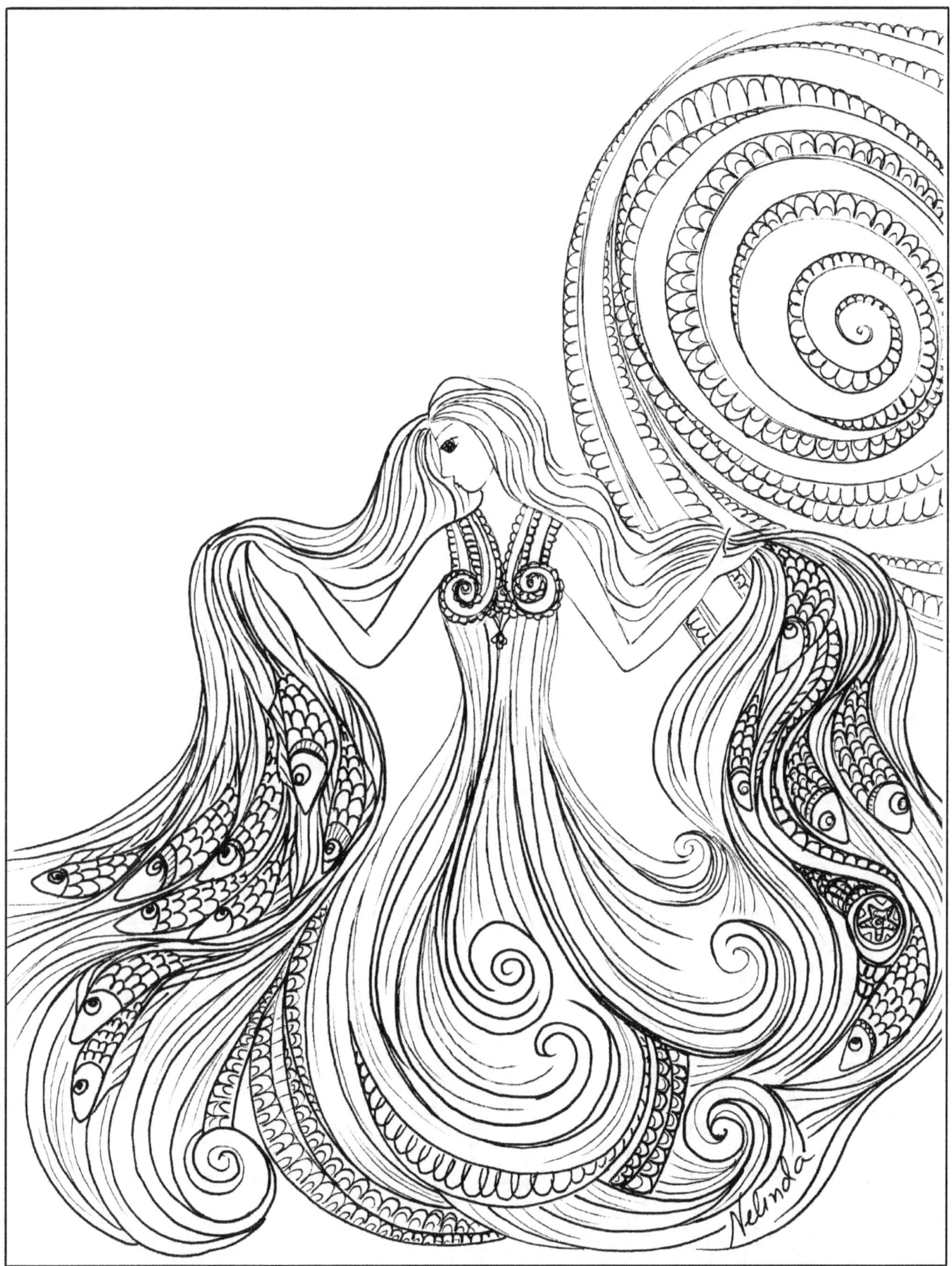

Hoy – Orkney Islands. A mermaid was sighted on September 13, 1913. Reports say a woman rose three feet from the sea. She wore a shawl around her shoulders and over her face.

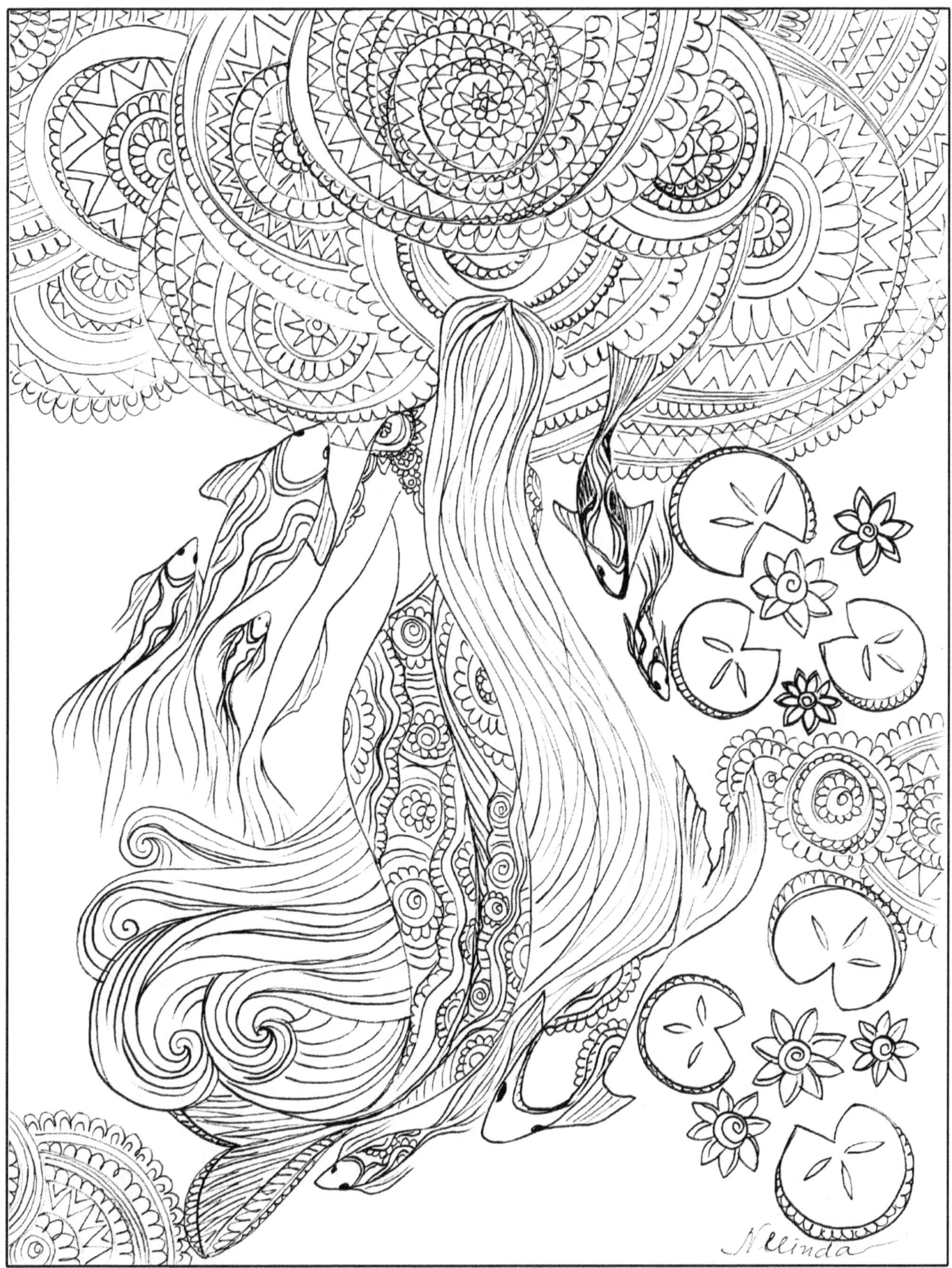

Magindara – Phillipines. Said to eat adult humans, these vicious mermaids do not harm children. During a full moon, Bulan descended from the sky to swim with the mermaids, who protected him from sea monsters.

www.ronesaaveela.com

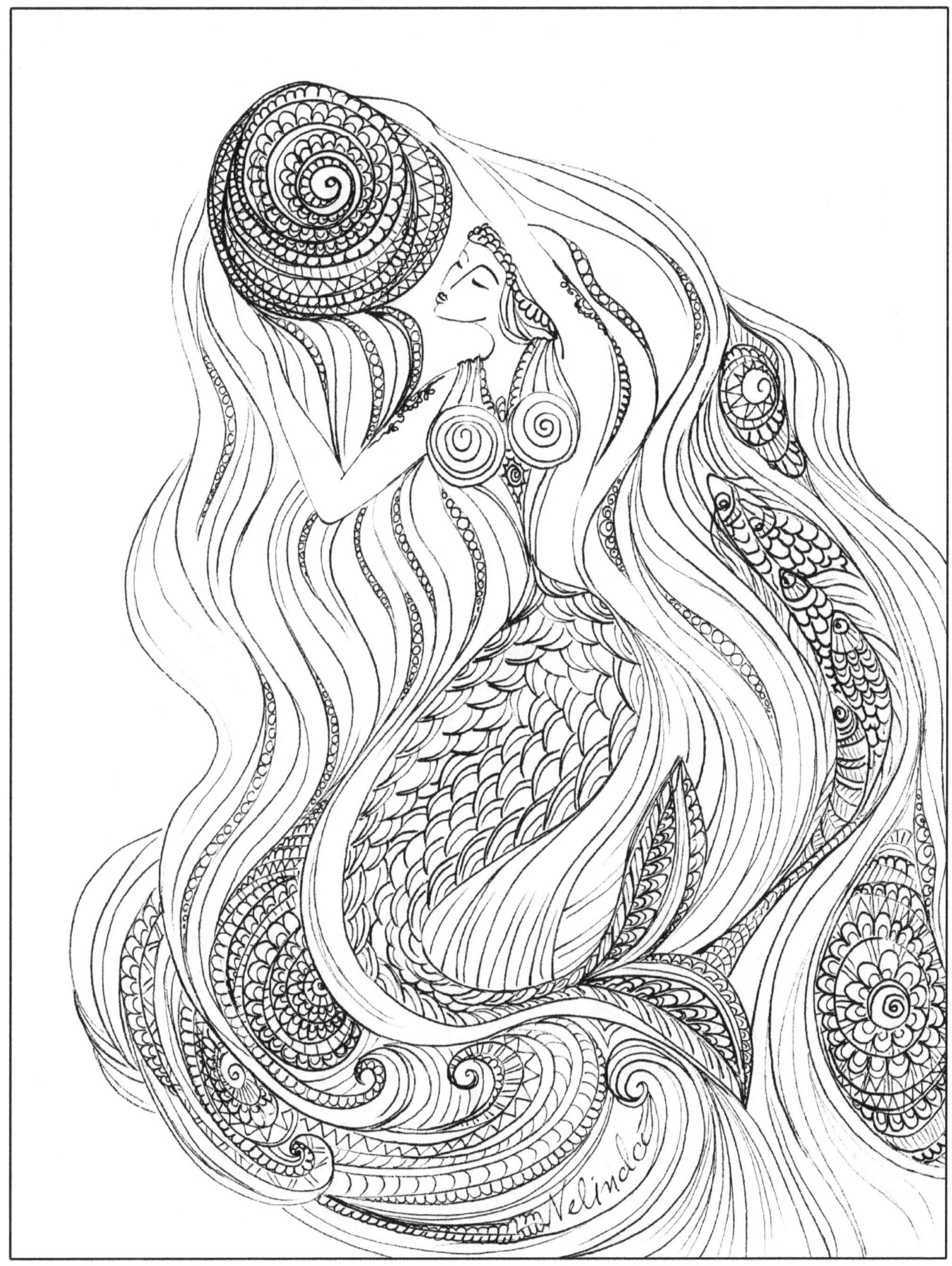

St. Murgen – Ireland. Tired of living by herself for many years, a mermaid was baptized so she could gain a soul. Told she could die immediately or live another 300 years before going to heaven, she chose death and became a saint.

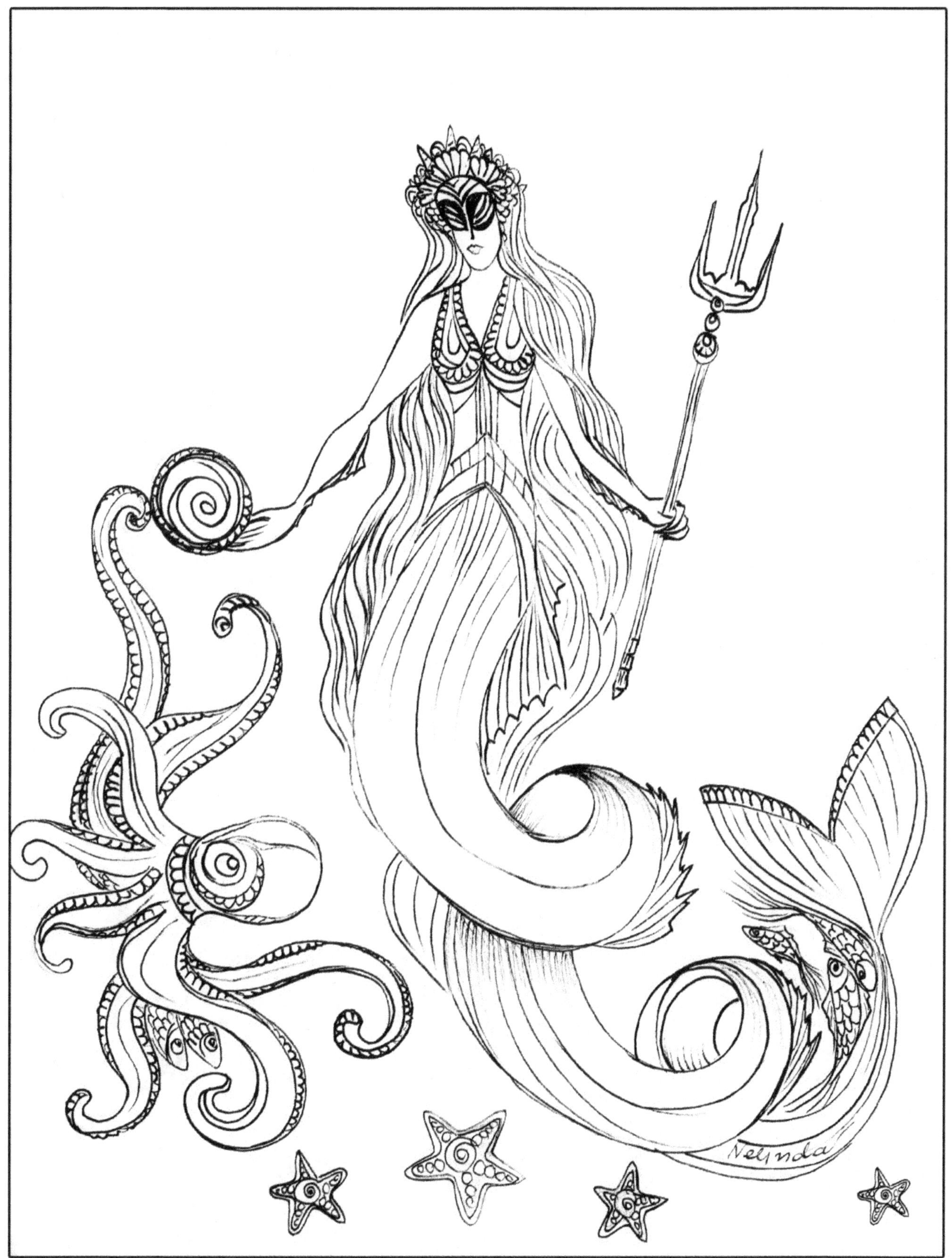

Nyai Roro Kidul – Indonesia. Cursed by a jealous harem, the daughter of a Pajajaran ruler became filthy and ugly and was forced from her home because she brought bad luck. She jumped into the Indian Ocean to cure herself and became a mermaid.

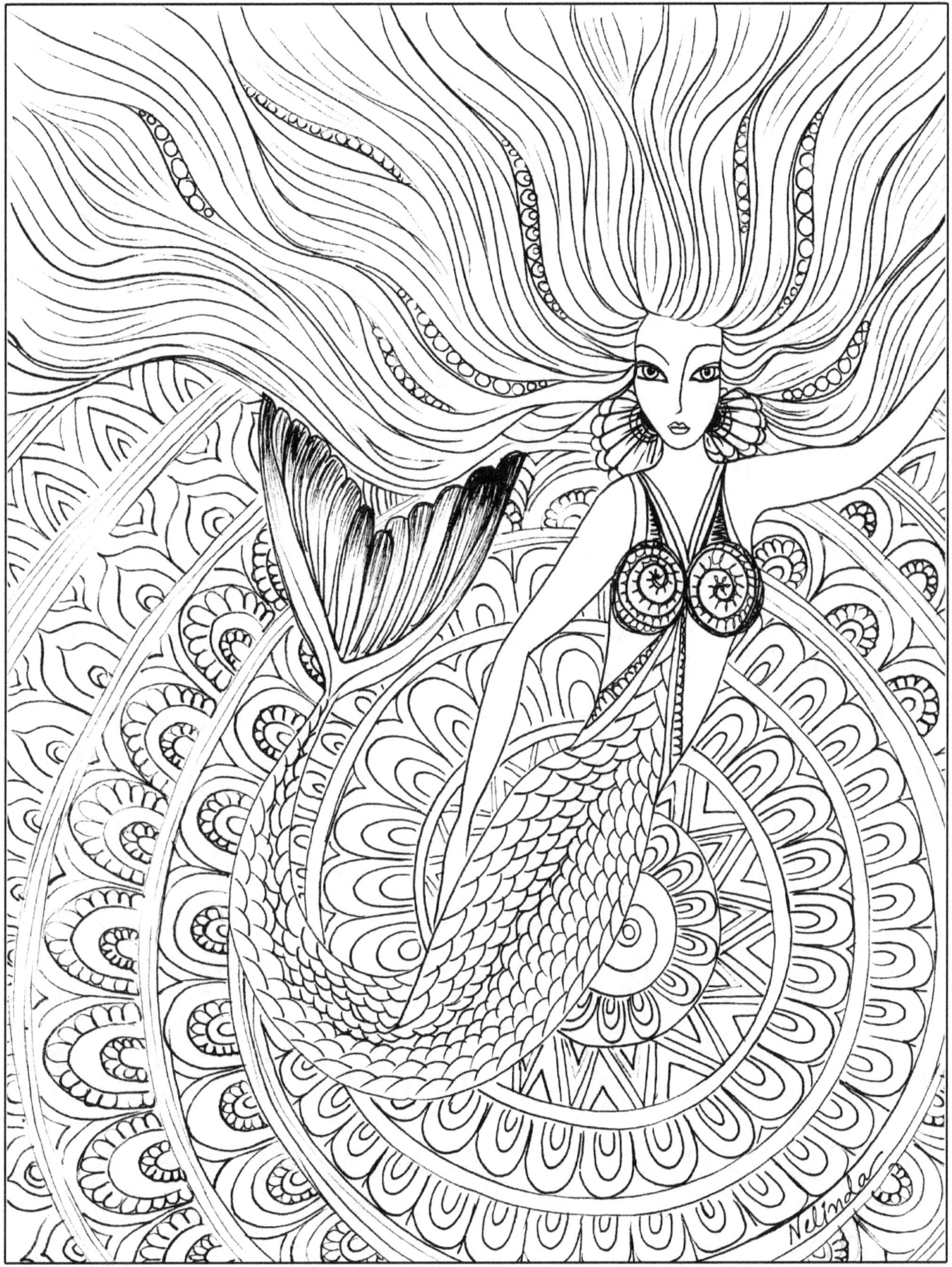

Olokun – West Africa. The Goddess of the Bottom of the Ocean, the Goddess of Death, Rebirth, and Renewal. She knows and guards the secrets of the past, present, and future.

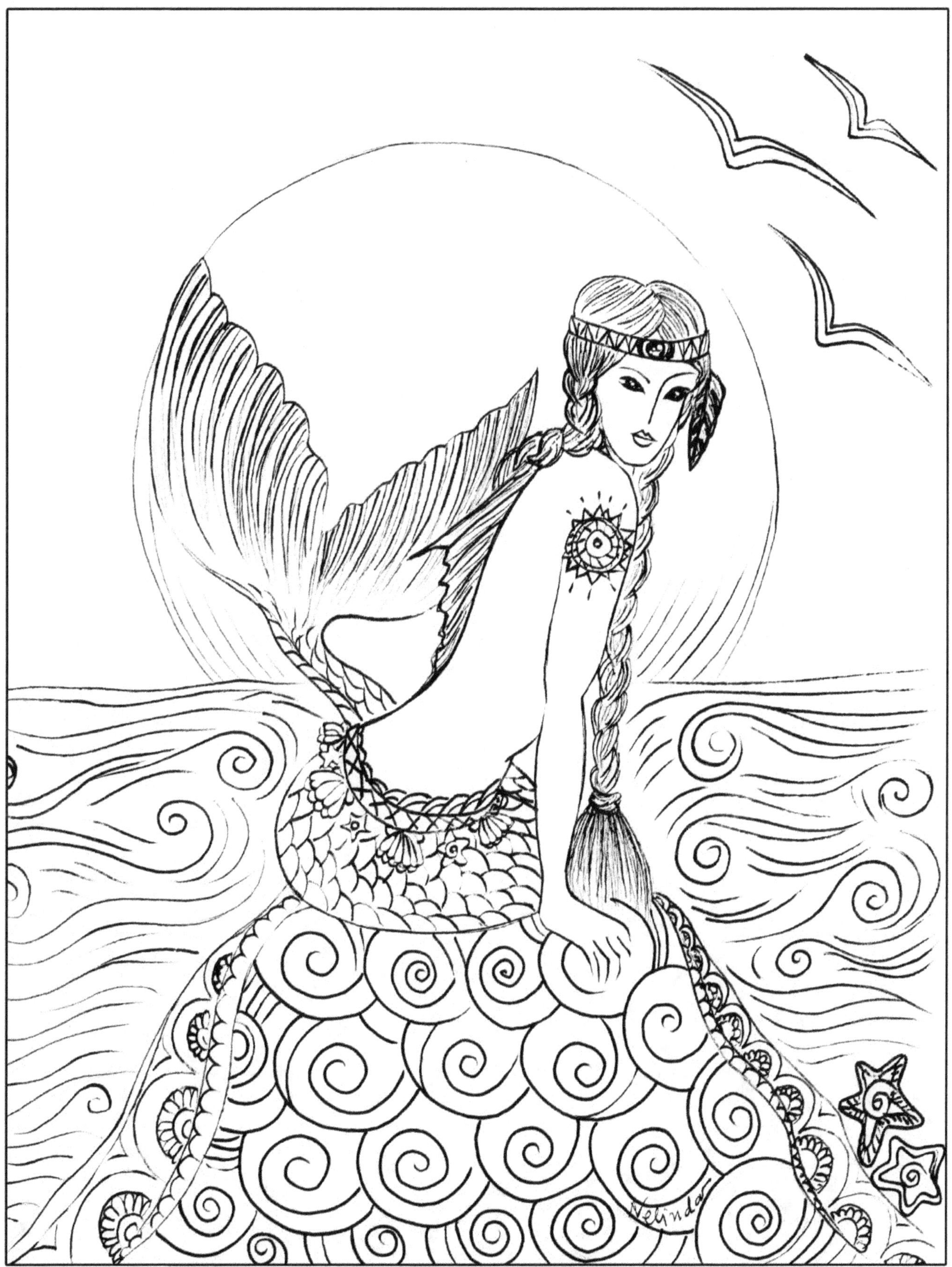

Squant – Native American. This sea-giantess wore her hair braided. She lived in an undersea cave and tried to lure men there. When the warrior Maushop would not follow her, she stirred up a storm.

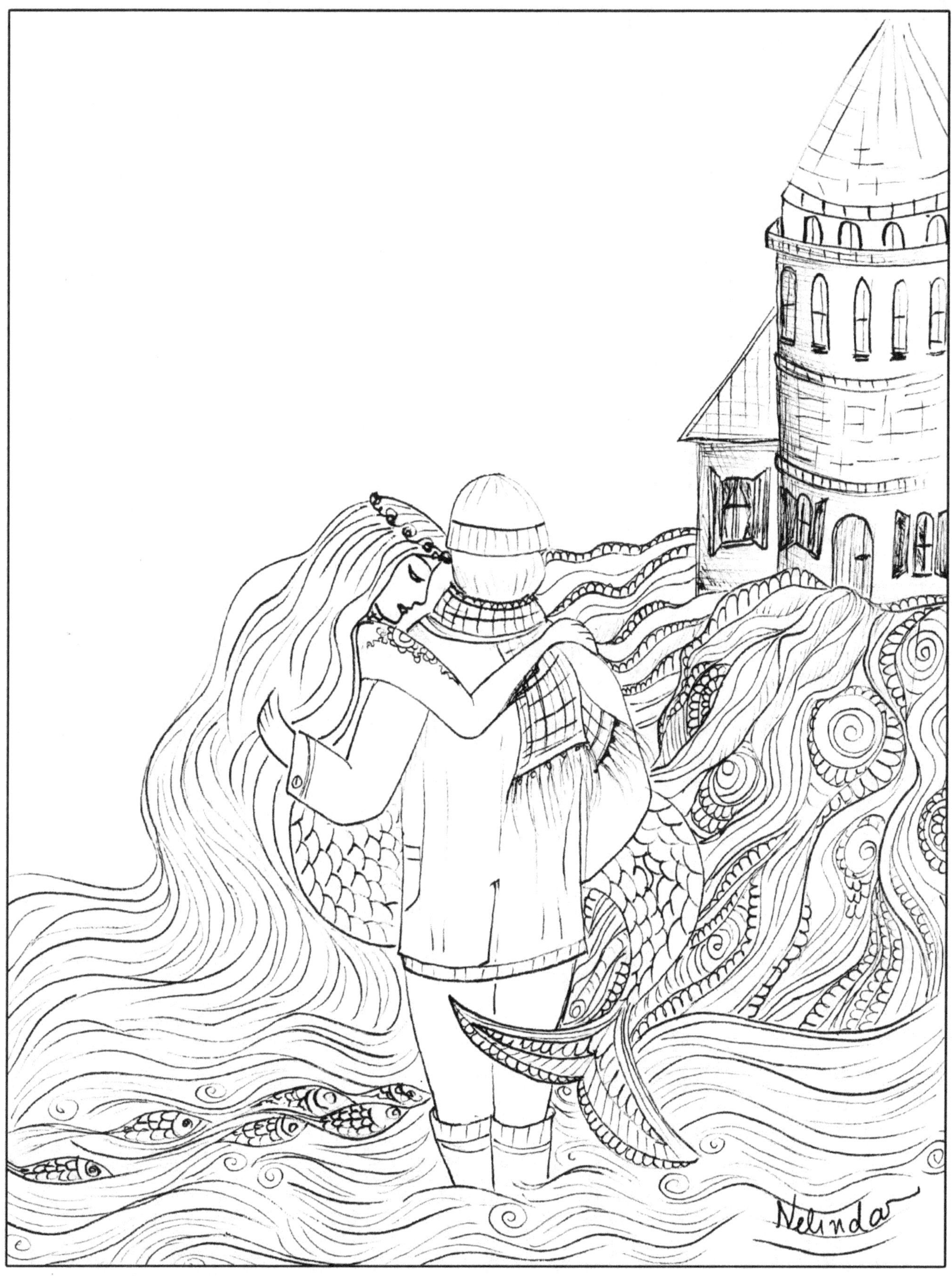

Merrymaids – Cornwall. An old man of Cury named Lutey rescued a mermaid who was stranded by rocks when the tide went out. When he carried her back to sea, she gave him her golden comb and also the power to do good for others.

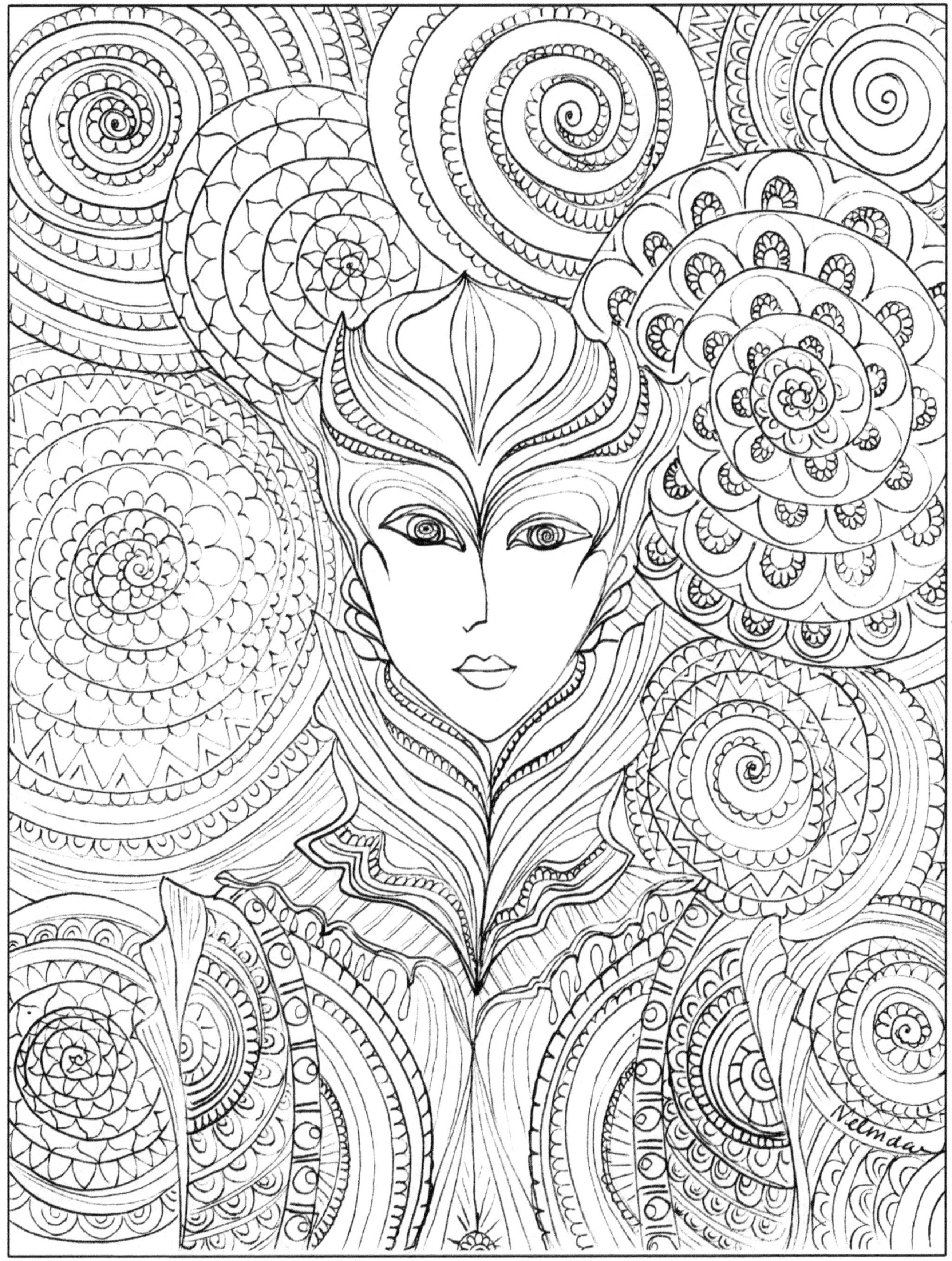

Nommo – Mali. These were the first beings the sky god Amma created. They gave the Dogon tribes their knowledge of astronomy.

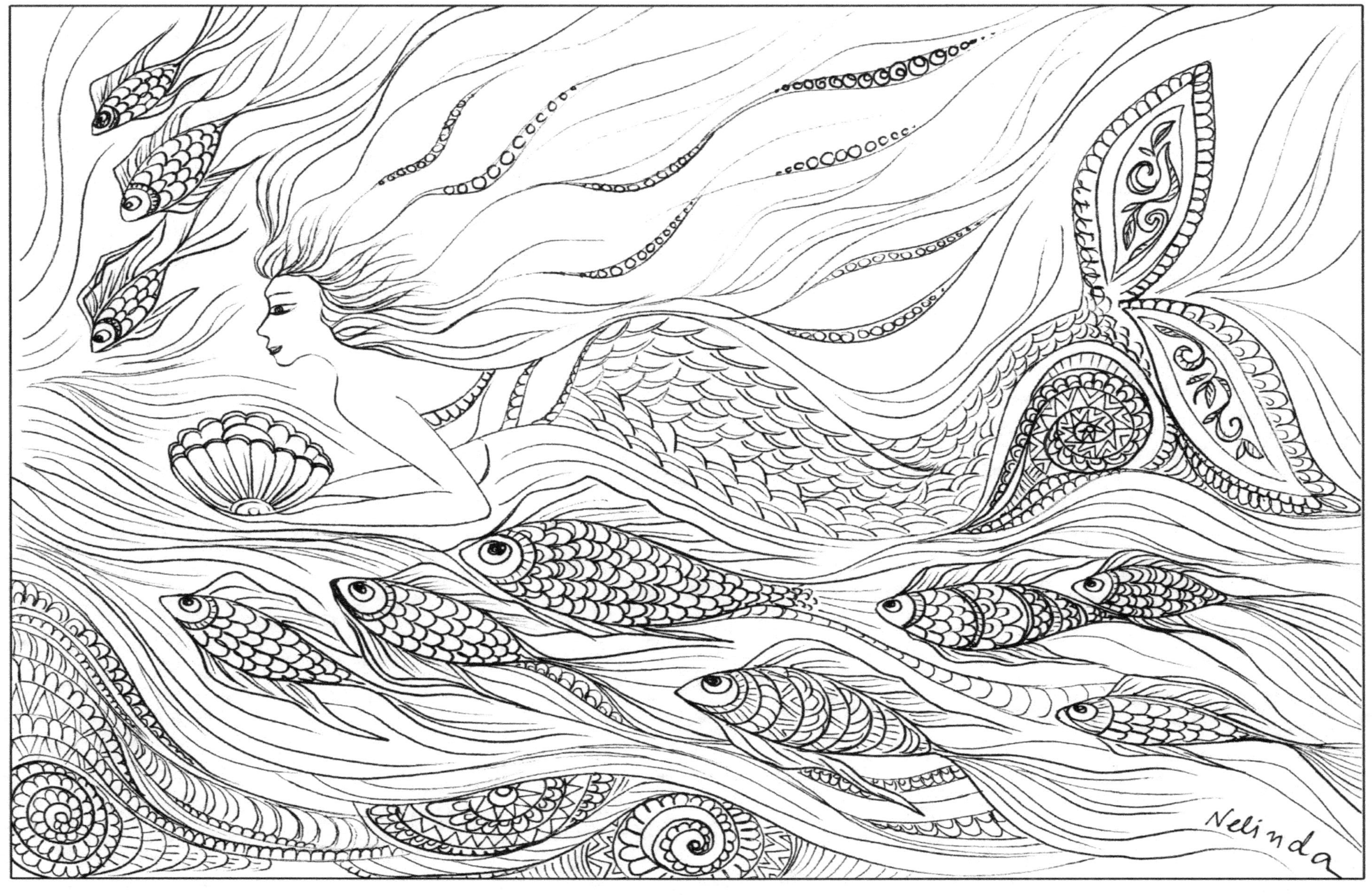

Sirena – Guam. Sirena loved swimming. One day she forgot to collect coconut shells. Her mother cursed her saying she should become a fish since she loved the water so much. Her grandmother added, "But leave the part of her that belongs to me."

www.ronesaavela.com

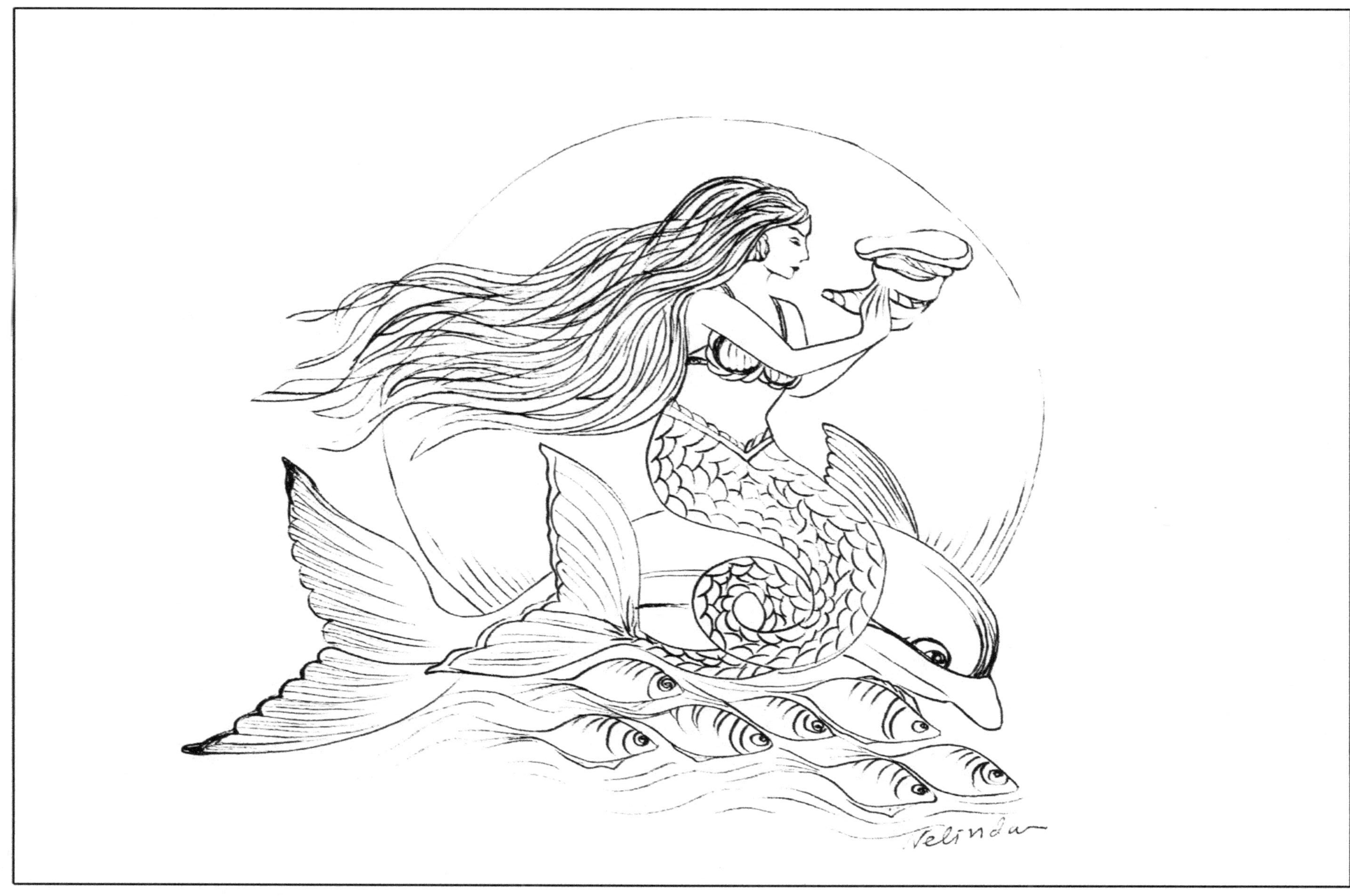

Natasha of the Sea – Ukraine. Tremsin set out to capture lost items for the haughty Natasha—first her coral necklace, then her wild horses—before he could capture her heart.

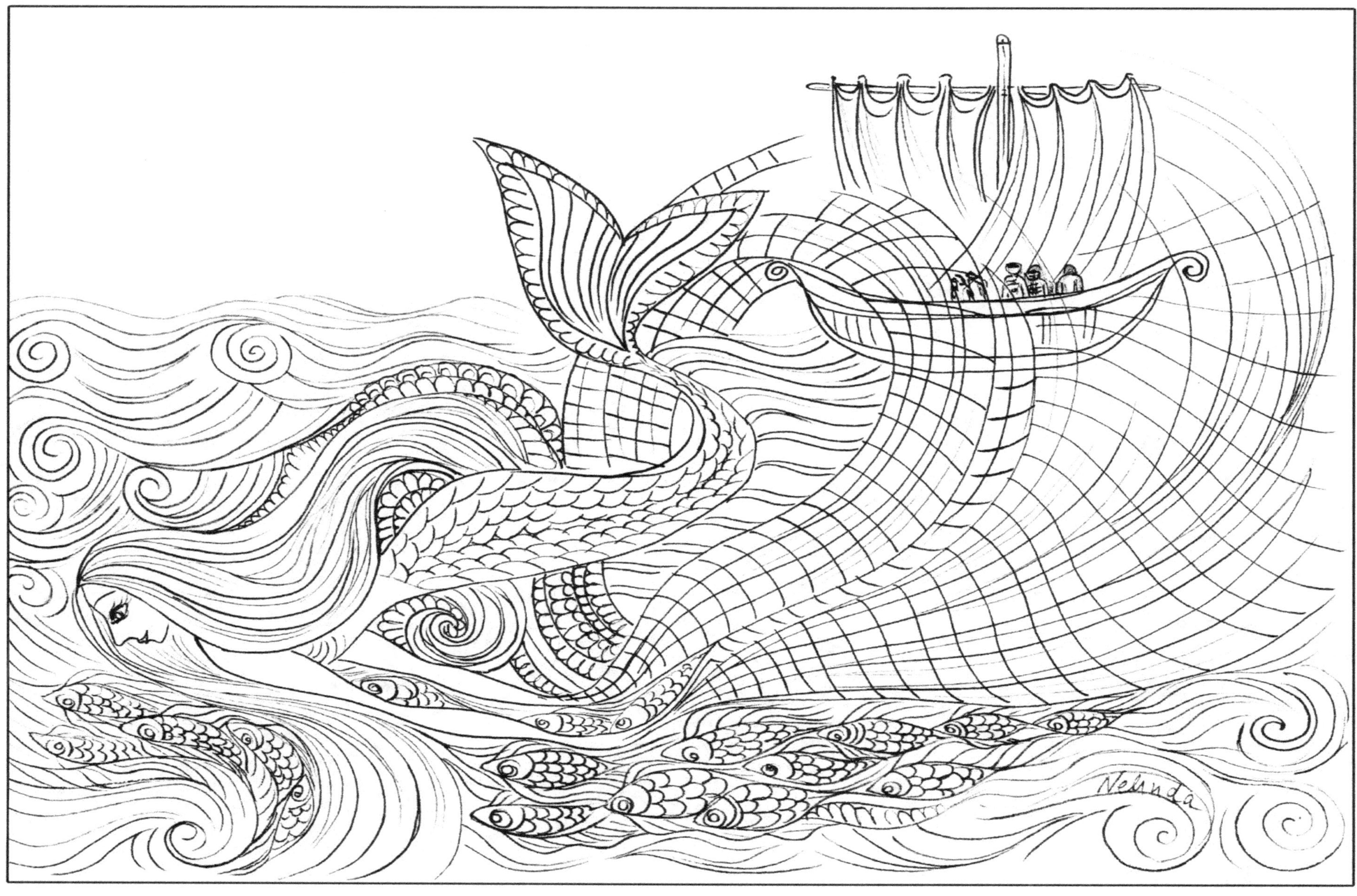

Rán – Scandinavia. A sea goddess who captured sailors in a huge net and brought them to her palace, where she fed them lobsters.

www.ronesaavela.com

About the Author

Ronesa Aveela is "the creative power of two." Two authors that is. The main force behind the work, the creative genius, was born in Bulgaria and moved to the US in the 1990s. She grew up with stories of wild Samodivi, Kikimora, the dragons Zmey and Lamia, Baba Yaga, and much more. She's a freelance artist and writer. She likes writing mystery romance inspired by legends and tales. In her free time, she paints. Her artistic interests include the female figure, Greek and Thracian mythology, folklore tales, and the natural world interpreted through her eyes. She is married and has two children.

Her writing partner was born and raised in the New England area. She has a background in writing and editing, as well as having a love of all things from different cultures. She's learned so much about Bulgarian culture, folklore, and rituals, and writes to share that knowledge with others.

Connect with Us!

Social Media: Website/Blog | Newsletter | Facebook | Twitter | Instagram | Pinterest | Goodreads | Bookbub | LinkedIn | YouTube |

Promo products: Redbubble

Ronesa's Books

Fiction
Mystical Emona: Soul's Journey
The Unborn Hero of Dragon Village
Zmeykovo (Bulgarian version of *The Unborn Hero of Dragon Village*)
La profezia del Villaggio del Drago (Italian version of *The Unborn Hero of Dragon Village*)

Nonfiction
Light Love Rituals: Bulgarian Myths, Legends, and Folklore
A Study of Household Spirits of Eastern Europe
A Study of Rusalki – Slavic Mermaids of Eastern Europe
A Study of Vodyanoy – Water Spirit of Eastern Europe
    (free gift when you sign up for Ronesa's newsletter at https://dl.bookfunnel.com/1rq3ku0fa9)
Skitnikut – usmivki I sulzi: Rasmisleniata na edin bulgarski emigrant (Bulgarian version of *The Wanderer*)
The Wanderer – A Tear and a Smile: Reflections of an Immigrant (available March 2020)

Children's short stories, activity & coloring books
Baba Treasure Chest series
The Christmas Thief
The Miracle Stork
Born From the Ashes
Mermaid's Gift
Baba Treasure Chest: A Collection of Modern Bulgarian Tales (contains all four short stories)

Coloring Books
Mermaids Around the World
More Mermaids Around the World
Little Zoi

Cookbook
Mediterranean & Bulgarian Cuisine: 12 Easy Traditional Favorites